COLLINS LIVING HISTORY

The World of Islam
up to 1500s

Fiona Macdonald

Series editor: Christopher Culpin

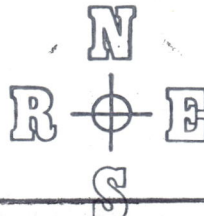

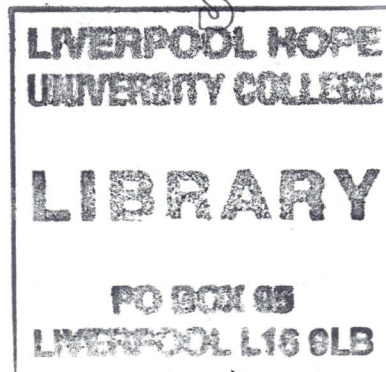

CollinsEducational

An imprint of HarperCollinsPublishers

Contents

attainment target 1

Questions aimed at this attainment target find out how much you know and understand about the past. Some questions are about how things were different in history: not only people's food, or clothes but their beliefs too. Others are about how things change through history, sometimes quickly, sometimes slowly, sometimes a little, sometimes a lot. Other questions ask you to explain why things were different in the past, and why changes took place.

attainment target 2

This attainment target is about understanding what people say about the past. Historians, as well as lots of other people, try to describe what the past was like. Sometimes they say different things. This attainment target is about understanding these differences and why they occur.

attainment target 3

This attainment target is about historical sources and how we use them to find out about the past. Some questions are about the historical evidence we can get from sources. Others ask you about how valuable this evidence might be.

Introduction

This book looks at the MEDIEVAL Muslim world, from around AD 570 to 1530. The 'Muslim world' means lands governed by Muslim rulers (one is shown below) where people followed the faith of Islam.

The men and women we shall be studying lived a long time ago, and their lives were different from ours in many ways. One major difference was the importance of religion. Religious leaders and laws were powerful, and everyone who could, gave money to religious charities. People believed in a life after death, when good behaviour would be rewarded and bad behaviour punished.

Muslims were not alone in these beliefs. People of many faiths shared similar ideas, and gave time and money to religious causes. Of course, some people had doubts, or preferred magic and superstition, while a few ignored religion altogether. But the teachings of Islam affected everyone who lived in the Muslim world, and gave birth to a rich and fascinating civilisation.

To Europe

To North Africa

ARAL SEA

BLACK SEA

CASPIAN SEA

Constantinople

BYZANTINE EMPIRE

MEDITERRANEAN SEA

Tigris

Euphrates

Damascus

Jerusalem

SASSANIAN EMPIRE

Nile

Medina

ARABIA

Mecca

RED SEA

KEY

Mountains

Desert areas

Main trade routes

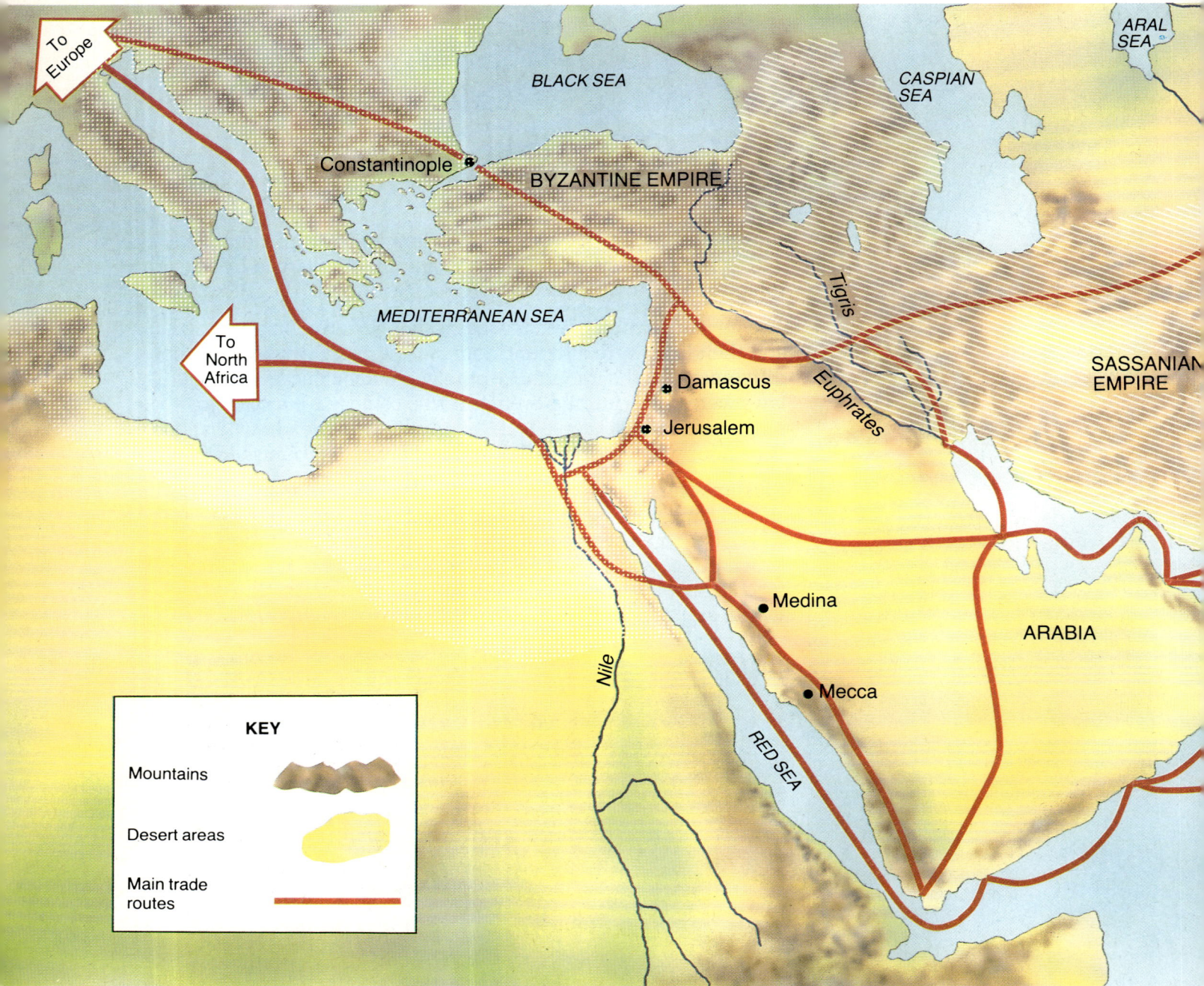

Lands of the Middle East in AD 600.

As you read through this book and study the sources, you will find out about the teachings of the Islamic faith. You will also discover how this faith spread rapidly from its beginnings in the Arabian cities of Mecca and Medina to the surrounding lands of the Middle East, and far beyond. The map above centres on the Muslim homeland of Arabia, where the message of Islam was first received.

By looking at the timeline opposite, you can discover some of the major events in nearly 1,000 years of Muslim history. During that period, Muslim states flourished in southern Europe, Spain, India, Asia and Africa. The evidence that survives from these states illustrates the richness and variety of the medieval Muslim world.

Map labels:
To China

Oxus

Indus

ARABIAN SEA

To India

N

0   800 km

A.D.

TIMELINE

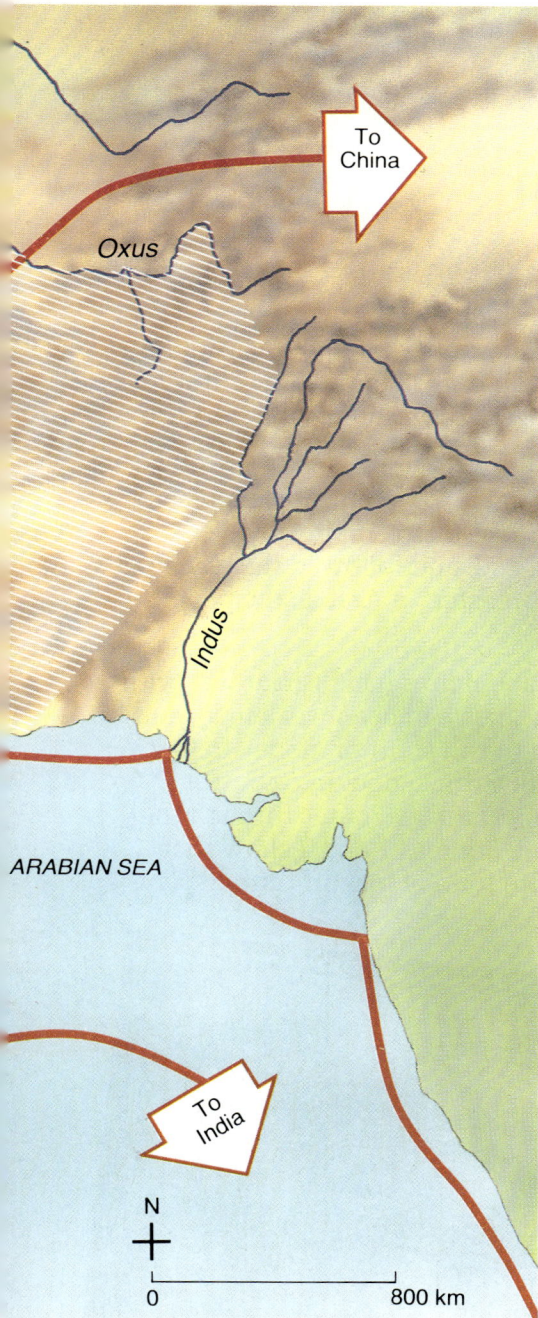

630–750
MUSLIM
EXPANSION

750–1055
RULE OF
THE ABBASID
CALIPHS

1096–1191
CRUSADER
WARS

1220–1260
MONGOL
INVASIONS

1453–1550
RISE OF
THE OTTOMAN
EMPIRE

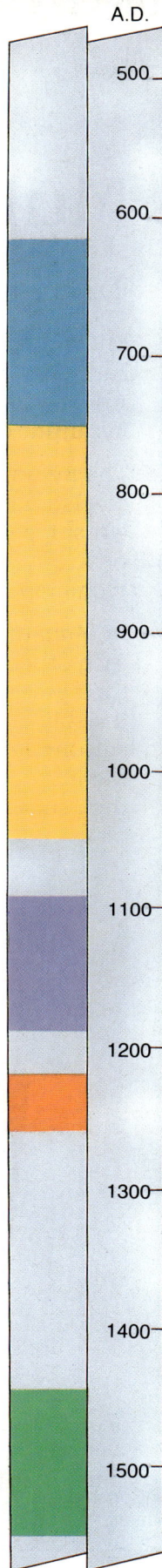

500

600

700

800

900

1000

1100

1200

1300

1400

1500

around 570
Birth of Muhammad

622
Flight from Mecca to Medina

632
Muhammad dies

711
Muslim rule established in
southern Spain

762
City of Baghdad founded

1057
Mahmud of Ghazni founds first
Muslim empire in Afghanistan
and northern India

1187
Muslim troops led by Saladin
recapture Jerusalem

1260
Mongols halted at battle of Ain Jalut

1299
Ottoman Turks establish a new
Muslim state in Turkey

1453
Ottoman troops capture
Constantinople

1529
Ottoman troops reach Vienna

Muhammad's world

Two great empires

Muhammad lived in Arabia, a hot, dry, dusty land in the Middle East. As you can see from the map on page 4, in the 6th century Arabia was overshadowed by two very powerful neighbours: the Byzantine empire and the Sassanian empire.

The Byzantine empire, with its capital in Constantinople (present-day Istanbul) was Christian. In the Sassanian empire, people worshipped Ahura Mazda, the sun-god, and followed the teachings of an ancient philosopher called Zoroaster. In Arabia, the people worshipped several different gods.

In Muhammad's time, the two great empires had been at war with each other for many years. Their armies had been weakened, and their governments were beginning to run short of money to pay the soldiers. Even so, they were still strong enough to control surrounding territories and the important sea routes through the Mediterranean and the Persian Gulf. Sources 1 and 2 show that their rulers were proud, wealthy and fond of magnificent display.

AIMS

In this unit we will look at the life of the PROPHET Muhammad, who lived in Arabia from around AD 570 to 632. Muhammad believed that he was a messenger sent by God, to teach people the right way to live. We will find out how Muhammad's message from God became the foundation for a new religion. It was called ISLAM, an Arabic word which means 'submission to God'. We will also see how this religion brought great changes in Arabia.

SOURCE 1
This magnificent solid gold plate was made for the Sassanian emperors some time during the 6th and 7th centuries. The magical creature shown on it was a sign of good fortune.

SOURCE 2
Mosaic showing the Byzantine Emperor Constantine IV handing over a document. It contained details of a gift he was making to the Church.

SOURCE 3
Life in the Arabian desert today,
where Bedouin families still lead
a nomadic life.

SOURCE 4
A busy town market in Yemen.
Many of the streets and houses in
these towns are built in the
traditional style.

Life in the Arabian desert

Arabia was no match for these empires. The
Arabian people had no single leader, but were
divided into a number of tribes who often fought
fierce wars against each other. They valued
justice and honour more than peace and safety.
Many of the tribes were NOMADS: they travelled
across the desert seeking food and water for the
camels, sheep and goats which moved with
them. Source 3 shows Bedouin people who still
live as nomads in Arabia today.

Trading and town life

Not all Arabians continued their traditional life
in the desert. Some people began to settle in
towns like the one shown in Source 4. In these
towns they worked at different crafts or became
merchants and shopkeepers.

As the map on page 4 shows, several
important trade routes passed close to Arabia
and Arabian merchants could grow rich by
buying and selling. Towns such as Mecca and
Siraf were famous for their markets filled with
goods from distant lands. Local craftsmen
produced fine leatherwork and perfumes.

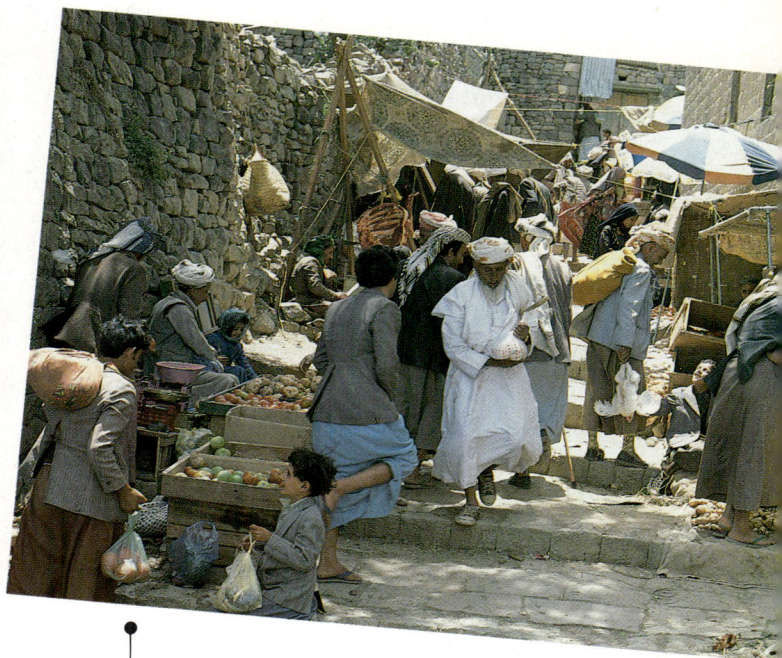

These changes in their way of life made many
Arabians feel uneasy. They feared that the old
standards of pride, honour and endurance were
being ignored. The town-dwellers and the
merchants seemed to be interested only in the
comforts of town life and in making money.

'The fiercest in heat and drought, and with the most
palm trees, is Arabia.'

SOURCE 5
From a description by a 10th
century Arab geographer.

Write down three ways in which life in a town like the
one in Source 4 might be different from life in the
desert. You could think about the following: homes and
housing, health, diet, clothing, number of friends and
standards of living.

> 'He was of medium height, inclined to slimness, with a large head and broad shoulders . . . His hair and beard were thick and black, not altogether straight but slightly curled. His hair reached midway between his ears and his shoulders and his beard was of a length to match. He had a noble breadth of forehead . . . His eyes were usually said to have been black, but (some early writers) describe them as brown. His nose was large and slightly hooked and his mouth was wide and finely shaped . . . His skin was white, but tanned by the sun . . .'

SOURCE 6
Descriptions of Muhammad made during his lifetime, and collected by a modern writer.

SOURCE 7
Mount Hira, outside Mecca. Muhammad received his first message from God in a cave on this mountainside.

The Prophet Muhammad

In about AD 570, a baby boy was born to a poor woman called Aminah who lived in Mecca. She named him 'Muhammad' which means 'highly praised'. Her husband had only recently died, so other members of her family helped her to bring up the child.

Aminah belonged to the powerful Quraysh tribe. It was the tribe's duty to protect the sacred shrine at Mecca, called the 'House of Prayer'. At this time, the shrine was filled with IDOLS – stones and statues – which were worshipped by the Arabian people.

As a young man, Muhammad started to work for one of his uncles, a travelling merchant. He was good at his job. When his uncle died, Muhammad soon found new work helping a wealthy widow named Khadija to run her business. Khadija was also a merchant and Muhammad went travelling, buying and selling for her. After a while, they married, and worked happily as partners for many years. Their business grew and prospered.

Muhammad was well known among the citizens of Mecca for his honesty and fairness, and for giving wise advice. He became known as 'al-Amin' which means 'the reliable' or 'the honest one'. Early writers said that Muhammad had a 'luminous' or 'radiant' expression – they could tell he was a holy man.

The vision in the cave

As he grew older, Muhammad began to spend time away from his business in Mecca. Not far from the city, there was a cave in the desert where he went to find peace (see Source 7). He wanted time to think and pray, and to feel closer to God. One night, he became certain that something extraordinary had happened. He returned home and told Khadija how he had seen an angel. The angel had brought him a message from God and commanded him to repeat it to the people of Mecca.

It was the first of many messages Muhammad was convinced he had received. Faithfully, he memorised them all and repeated them to his friends. In the years which followed, they were written down and collected together to form a book. This book is known today as the QUR'AN, which means 'reading' or 'recitation' (Source 8).

> Recite in the name of thy Lord who created . . .

SOURCE 8
From the Qur'an (96:1). The first message Muhammad received from God was to recite or repeat everything the angel told him.

Muhammad spent the rest of his life telling people about God's message. He encouraged them to worship the one true God, and to live according to God's commands. In Mecca, people began to follow Muhammad's example. They became known as MUSLIMS and formed a close, co-operative community. Today, about one person in five throughout the world is a Muslim and follows the religion of Islam.

Source 6 describes in words what the Prophet Muhammad looked like. Islam teaches that it is wrong to make pictures or statues of living creatures, since God is the only creator. Most Muslim artists do not draw pictures of people and animals. Instead they create wonderful patterns and designs, often based on the Arabic script.

> Look at Sources 9 and 11 below. Write down two ways in which these pages from the Qur'an have been made beautiful to look at.

The flight from Mecca

Muhammad's teaching (see, for example, Source 10), angered many of the people of Mecca. They attacked him and his companions, and forced them to leave the city. In AD 622, the Muslims made the journey to Medina, another town about 350 kilometres to the north of Mecca. It was a special journey, known as the HIJRA, and in the Islamic calendar, all years are counted from this date.

The people of Medina welcomed Muhammad, and within a few years he became accepted as an important religious leader. During this time there were several battles between Muslim troops and raiding parties sent from Mecca. The Muslims won most of these battles. They believed this was because God was on their side.

> Increasing, multiplied wealth is your besetting preoccupation, all the way to the tomb. But soon you will realise . . .
>
> *besetting preoccupation:* all you think about

SOURCE 10
From the Qur'an (102:1-2).

SOURCE 9
Page from a 9th century Qur'an.

SOURCE 11
A 16th century Qur'an manuscript from Egypt.

From Medina to Mecca

In Medina, the Muslims tried their best to follow the teachings of the Qur'an. They prayed together and listened to Muhammad's preaching. The first MOSQUE was built here at Medina. Later, mosques were built elsewhere in Arabia and throughout the Muslim world (see Source 14).

> God commands justice, well-doing and generosity towards your kinsfolk. . .
>
> *kinsfolk:* relations; also, in this source, fellow-Muslims

SOURCE 13
From the Qur'an (16.90).

> Do not envy one another; do not inflate prices; do not hate one another; do not turn away from one another; do not undercut one another; but be like brothers, O servants of Allah. A Muslim is the brother of a Muslim: he neither oppresses him nor does he fail him; he neither lies to him nor holds him in contempt . . .
>
> *Allah:* the one true God
> *oppress:* treat unfairly, or cruelly

SOURCE 12
This is part of a famous HADITH, one of Muhammad's sayings. Hadith were remembered by people who lived close to Muhammad. Later on, they were collected and written down by Muslim scholars.

The conquest of Mecca

Towards the end of his life, Muhammad decided to revisit Mecca. He wanted to get rid of the idols in the House of Prayer, and make it a place where Muslims could worship the one true God of Islam.

In 630, Muhammad led a strong army of Muslims to Mecca. The Meccans felt outnumbered, and they surrendered without a fight. Unusually for the time, Muhammad did not punish his opponents – even though they had once forced him to leave his home city. Instead, he brought presents for the people of Mecca, to show that he forgave them, and wanted to live in peace with them.

Purifying the House of Prayer

Muhammad believed that the House of Prayer in Mecca had been built by the Prophet Abraham and his son Ishmael, thousands of years ago. They, too, had worshipped the one true God, but after their deaths, the House of Prayer had fallen into the hands of people who worshipped many different gods. After his conquest of Mecca, Muhammad's first action was to remove all the idols from the House of Prayer.

1 Which types of people is Muhammad talking to in Sources 12 and 13? Neighbours? Business people? Families? Everyone?

2 Use Source 16 to work out a list of criticisms that were made of Muhammad in his lifetime.

3 Source 17 shows Muhammad's grave as it looks today. What does this tell you about Muslim respect for the Prophet Muhammad?

SOURCE 14
Bilhal's Mosque, Mecca, named after one of the Prophet's companions.

Your kinsman . . . is not out of his mind. He saw truly . . .

Your kinsman has not been led astray, nor is he under a delusion. He does not speak some whim of his own . . . The vision he saw in his heart he does not deny.

Are they spreading it around that he has concocted it – this Qur'an?

concocted: made it up

SOURCE 16
These extracts from the Qur'an (81:22, 53:2-10 and 52:33) all refer to Muhammad. They defend the Prophet and his faith against criticisms made at the time.

SOURCE 15
The Ka'aba, at the centre of the Great Mosque in Mecca.

The House of Prayer contained a holy stone known as the Black Stone. Muslims believe that this stone was placed by angels in the foundations of the original House of Prayer. In Source 15 you can see the House of Prayer as it is today. It is called the KA'ABA. The cube-shaped building contains the Black Stone. The Ka'aba has black silk curtains, embroidered in gold.

Death of the Prophet

Shortly before he died, Muhammad led a great PILGRIMAGE of Muslims from Medina and elsewhere to the House of Prayer at Mecca. The pilgrims were able to praise God and give thanks that they could worship at the ancient holy site.

Many Meccan citizens adopted the faith of Islam and decided to follow the Muslim way of life. Muhammad became the respected leader of this growing community. By now, the teachings of Islam and news of Muhammad's peaceful entry into Mecca had spread throughout Arabia. More and more people became Muslims, although, as Source 16 shows, there was still some opposition to Muhammad and the faith of Islam.

Muhammad died in 632, in Medina. He was mourned by all Muslims, and by many non-Muslims as well. He was buried in a simple grave, in his home.

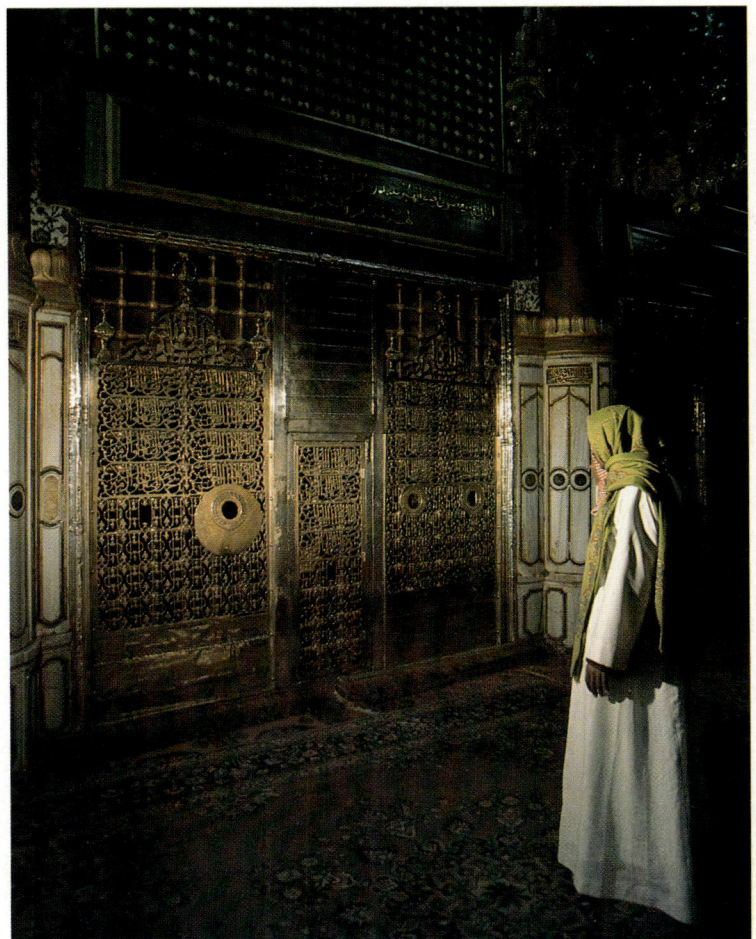

SOURCE 17
The solid gold gates surrounding Muhammad's tomb.

The first Muslims

We have seen how Muhammad and the message he preached attracted a number of followers. These men and women had to face criticism and abuse on account of their beliefs. They were attacked in Mecca, and finally had to leave their own homes to live in a strange city far away. What exactly did these first Muslims believe? What were the main points of the message Muhammad passed on to them?

The core of the Islamic faith can be summed up in the following words:

'There is no god but God, and Muhammad is the Messenger of God.'

Anyone – when Muhammad was alive, or even today – who makes this statement in public and in front of witnesses can be counted as a Muslim. Of course, Muslims believe that these words must also be said sincerely.

SOURCE 18
The 'five pillars' of Islam.

Fast (do not eat or drink in daylight hours) during the month of RAMADAN.

Perform the HAJJ: a special pilgrimage to the House of Prayer at Mecca.

Worship the One True God, and do not worship anyone or anything else. Respect the Prophet Muhammad as God's messenger.

SOURCE 19
This 13th century manuscript illustration from Baghdad shows a group of Muslims making the pilgrimage to Mecca.

A way of life

The rules for living a good life were set down in the Qur'an. They are very detailed, and they cover everything from how to go on a pilgrimage, to arranging a divorce, or carrying out business. The most important rules are known as the 'five pillars' of Islam, and they are described in Source 18.

In Islam, there is no distinction between religion and everyday life. Muslims should try to behave in a way that is pleasing to God in all that they do. God sees everything. He judges people according to how well or badly they have lived (see Source 20). The Qur'an therefore is a guide for all aspects of Muslim people's lives.

None of you truly believes until he wishes for his brother what he wishes for himself.

Let him who believes in Allah and the Last Day either speak good or keep silent . . . be generous to his neighbour . . . and be generous to his guest.

Last Day: Day of Judgement, or the end of the world, when Muslims believe that people will be rewarded or punished according to how they have lived.

SOURCE 20
Two hadith of the Prophet Muhammad.

Say your prayers five times a day, as instructed in the Qur'an.

Give a share of your income to help poor and needy people.

SOURCE 21
From a 17th century painting. After a period of fasting, these Muslims have gathered for a special evening meal.

A new community

Becoming Muslim changed people's lives completely. As well as trying to follow a new religion and new standards of behaviour, the first Muslims became part of a new, international community which soon spread far beyond the borders of Arabia. Muhammad taught that all Muslims were brothers in the sight of God, so Muslims were meant to support each other with friendship and help.

1 Study Source 18. What are the 'five pillars' of Islam? How do you think each affected the everyday lives of the early Muslims?

2 Source 19 shows a group of early Muslims making the pilgrimage to Mecca. In what ways do you think these gatherings supported and encouraged them in their faith?

3 Choose two other sources from this unit, one a picture, the other in words. Make a list of the difficulties historians might have in using them to discover what happened in 6th and 7th century Arabia.

ACTIVITY

Do this activity in pairs. You are two members of a family in 7th century Mecca. One of you is thinking of becoming a Muslim, the other does not agree. Write a short scene to explain your different views. You could act out this scene for the rest of the class.

Muhammad's place in history

For Muslims today, as well as those living in earlier centuries, Muhammad is much more than a great leader. He is the last true prophet, or messenger of God. Some Muslims might, therefore, feel insulted that historians should discuss Muhammad as if he were no different from other great leaders. We should understand and respect these views when we consider Muhammad's achievements.

Whether or not we believe that Muhammad was God's messenger, we can all admire him as a man of great honesty and courage. He held fast to his beliefs, even when this meant losing everything and living in exile. He was a successful teacher whose message brought the people of Arabia together and set very high standards of behaviour for all Muslims to follow.

SOURCE 23
Camel trains in the Sahara desert. Muslim merchants carried the message of Islam with them on journeys like these.

attainment target 1

1 Some of Muhammad's achievements are shown on page 15 opposite. Can you think of any more to add to the list?

2 How did Muhammad's message affect the lives of the following groups?
- merchants
- Meccans
- women
- non-Muslims
- people of the desert

3 Which aspects of the traditional Arabian way of life changed most, and which changed hardly at all?

4 Can you think of any problems that Muhammad's achievements may have caused?

Use the sources in this unit to help you.

'I do not weep for him, because I know that he has gone to a better place than this world. But I weep for the tidings from Heaven which have been cut off from us.'

better place: to Paradise
tidings: news and guidance

SOURCE 24
Comment made by Umm Ayman, Muhammad's devoted nurse, when she learned of his death. How can you tell from this that she had become a Muslim?

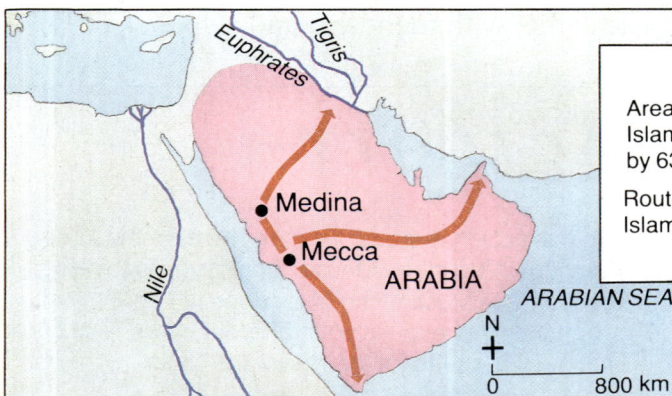

KEY

Area under Islamic influence by 632 AD

Routes of Islamic advance

SOURCE 22
Lands under Islamic influence at the death of Muhammad in 632.

'Treat the life and property of every Muslim as sacred.

Treat your wives well; they are your partners and helpers.

Beware of temptations leading you away from God.

All believers are brothers. Do not take anything from another Muslim unless he gives it to you freely.

Follow Muhammad's example, and the teachings of the Qur'an.

Worship God, say your prayers, fast during RAMADAN, give charity to poor people.

There will be no other prophet after Muhammad. Listen to his words, and pass them on to others.'

SOURCE 25
Main points of the 'farewell sermon' preached by Muhammad to pilgrims at Mecca, shortly before he died.

SOURCE 26
Pilgrims circling the Ka'aba, in Mecca.

Muhammad's achievements

- A new community of Muslims had grown up, based in Medina and Mecca. The Islamic faith spread from these cities to the borders of Arabia by the time of Muhammad's death, as you can see from Source 22.

- Muslims had been given a new set of rules by which to live. (After Muhammad's death, these were written down in the book called the Qur'an.)

- People had been encouraged to treat one another as brothers. Muhammad had taught men and women to treat one another with respect (see Source 25). Women's rights to their own property were made clear. (Of course, not all the people who became Muslims lived up to these high standards, just as not all Christians and Jews living in Europe and the Middle East at that time behaved in the way that their religious leaders taught them.)

- The Arabian people became united under one leader for the first time.

- Sincere Muslims believed in a life after death (see Source 24) where their good deeds would be rewarded and their bad deeds punished. This affected their behaviour.

- The House of Prayer at Mecca had become a place of pilgrimage for Muslims, who travelled there, following Muhammad's example.

- New rules to encourage fair trading among merchants had been introduced. Muslims were also encouraged to be clean, to be welcoming to strangers, and to be polite. Of course, not everyone obeyed these rules, but, when they were followed, they helped to make life more pleasant.

The spread of Islam

God's will

The first Muslims firmly believed that God had shown them the right way to live. They were also confident that God would help them to spread the message of Islam.

Even during Muhammad's lifetime, it had sometimes been necessary to fight in order to protect the first Muslims and their families. Muslim armies had already won several battles against troops from non-Muslim tribes elsewhere in Arabia. Now the Muslim commanders decided to face the mighty Byzantine and Sassanian empires. These SUPERPOWERS still controlled most of the lands surrounding Arabia, and threatened the safety of the Islamic heartland.

AIMS

In this unit we will look at the way Islam spread from its beginnings in 7th century Arabia to influence a vast territory stretching from the borders of China to the Atlantic coast of Spain. How did Muslim rulers govern such a large area? And what was life like for the people who lived under Muslim rule?

SOURCE 1

Lands brought under Muslim government between the mid 7th and mid 8th centuries.

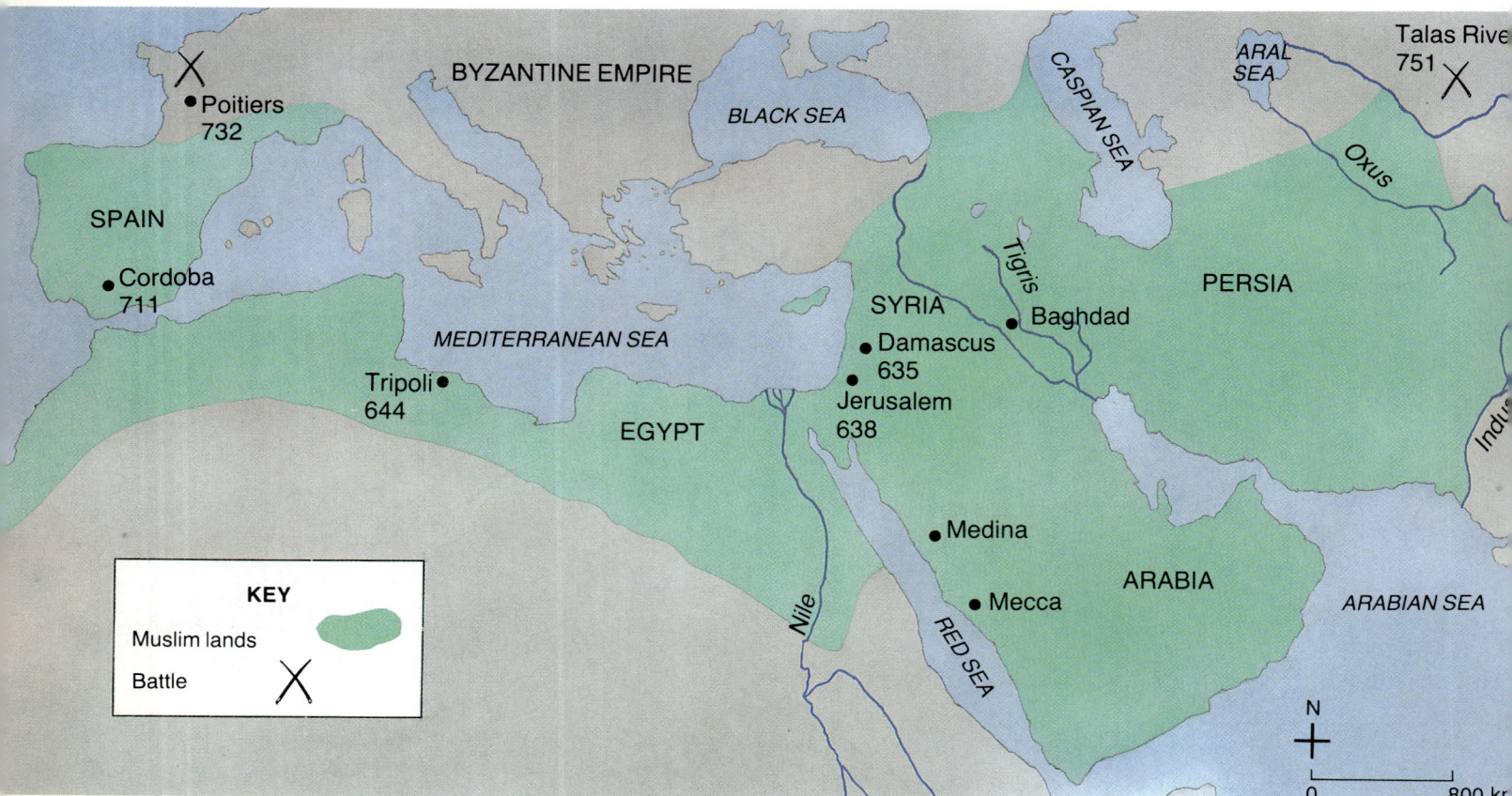

BYZANTINE EMPIRE

Talas River 751 X

ARAL SEA

Poitiers 732 X

BLACK SEA

CASPIAN SEA

Oxus

SPAIN

Cordoba 711

MEDITERRANEAN SEA

Tigris

PERSIA

Baghdad

SYRIA

Damascus 635

Jerusalem 638

Tripoli 644

EGYPT

Nile

Indus

Medina

ARABIA

ARABIAN SEA

Mecca

RED SEA

KEY

Muslim lands

Battle X

N

0   800 kr

SOURCE 2
Arabian troops on camels, armed with swords and lances. Camels could cover long distances over dry stony countryside without stopping for food and water. They were very useful to the Muslims in the early desert campaigns.

SOURCE 3
In countries where camels were not known, Muslim soldiers rode horses into battle. This 10th century drawing illustrates the speed of the horse and shows that its rider was well equipped, with a shield and long lance.

Muslim victories

Islamic troops quickly won a number of important victories. They advanced north into the two empires, and west into North Africa and Spain. They won a great battle at Talas River in Central Asia, where they defeated the armies of the emperor of China. Source 1 shows the huge area that the Muslims controlled by 751.

To people living at the time, this Muslim advance seemed almost like a miracle. In just over one hundred years, Muslim armies had brought Islamic rule to a large part of the known world. How had this happened? Sources 2 to 6 give some of the reasons for this success.

The Muslims were also delighted by the wealth their new territories brought them. The Muslims saw these riches as signs of God's favour. They felt encouraged to look for fresh victories.

> Permission is given to those who fight because they have been wronged, and indeed God is able to give them victory . . .

SOURCE 4
What message is being given to Muslims in this quotation from the Qur'an (22:39)?

> When God's help comes about, and conquest, and you have seen people come crowding to the religion of God, then sing the praise of your Lord and seek his forgiveness . . .

SOURCE 5
From the Qur'an (110:1-3).

> 'The inhabitants of Damascus (shall have) security for their lives, property and churches. Their city wall shall not be demolished, neither shall any Muslim be quartered in their houses. Thereunto we give the pact of Allah and the protection of his Prophet . . . So long as they pay the poll tax, nothing but good shall befall them.'

SOURCE 6
These were the terms of surrender set out by the Muslims when they conquered the city of Damascus in 635.

1 Use Sources 2 to 6 to explain why the Muslim armies were so successful.

2 How much of their success do you think was due to their religious beliefs, and how much to their military skill?

Travellers and traders

Islam spread in many peaceful ways as well. Muslim travellers and traders carried the faith to people living far away from the Islamic heartland of Arabia. Even in the days before Muhammad, Arab merchants travelled very long distances. They traded in goods produced in Middle Eastern countries and in luxury items from more distant lands. Arab travellers reached China, India and the eastern coast of Africa. Source 7 shows that Arabian coins were known and treasured in 8th century England.

Muslim merchants

During Muhammad's lifetime, a great many Arab merchants became Muslims. Naturally, they spoke about their new-found faith to the people they met on their journeys (see Sources 8 and 9). News of the religion spread to wherever Muslim merchants travelled. People in distant lands were impressed by the behaviour of Muslims who followed the teachings of the Qur'an. You can see from Source 10 that the Islamic faith became popular in parts of Europe too.

Source 11 shows that Muslim travellers were well received in other countries. At the same time, Muslim rulers also tried to attract people who they felt would be useful and productive citizens (see Source 12). Many of these settlers soon became members of the Muslim community. They also formed a link between their new Islamic countries and their non-Muslim homelands.

SOURCE 7
King Offa of England's copy of an Arab gold dinar.

SOURCE 8
This drawing comes from a 13th-century Arabian manuscript. It shows two Muslim merchants passing through a village.

SOURCE 9
KHANS, or guest houses, were built along the desert trading routes. They provided shelter and food for travellers, who could rest and exchange information. This picture shows a present-day khan in Turkey.

'The great city called Palermo is surrounded by a vast stone wall, tall and strong. Many merchants live there. The city has a great mosque, which was built as a Christian church shortly before the Conquest . . . The size of the city's population can be guessed from the large numbers of men who come to this mosque; I estimated that the congregation, when it was full, to be about 7,000 persons.

In Palermo and (nearby) Khalisa . . . there are more than 300 mosques, mostly in good condition . . . There are also mosques outside the city, surrounded by gardens . . . I have never seen so many mosques, except perhaps in Cordoba . . . I asked the reason for this and was told that the Sicilian people are so puffed up with pride that each of them wants to have his own mosque, to be used only by himself, his family, and their servants.'

SOURCE 10
From a description of Sicily written in 973. The island was under Muslim rule from 831 to 1090.

Peaceful alliances

Other people realised that it might be useful if they made alliances or co-operated with the Muslims. If they became CONVERTED to Islam, there were a number of practical advantages, as well as the spiritual strength of the new faith.

- They would be able to join a fast-growing community, in which they could rely on their fellow Muslims for help and support.

- They would be safe from attack, since the Muslim armies would not occupy another Muslim territory.

- They would be able to call on well-trained Muslim troops to defend them.

SOURCE 11
Muslim visitors being received by the King of Abyssinia (present-day Ethiopia) in 1306.

SOURCE 12
'An Invitation to Merchants' sent out by the Sultan of Egypt in about 1280.

'The Sultan (ruler) offers a genuine welcome to those who come to his realm, as to the Garden of Eden, by whatever gate they may choose to enter, from Iraq, from Persia, from Asia Minor, from the Hijaz (western Arabia), from India and from China. Whoever wishes to set forth – distinguished merchants, the men of great affairs, and the small traders – from the countries listed and also from those which have not been named, . . . let him come to . . . an earthly paradise for those who dwell in it, and a consolation for those who are far from their own homes . . .'

1 What does Source 10 tell us about the lives and beliefs of the Sicilian people of Palermo?

2 Why do you think the Sicilians built so many mosques? Think of at least two reasons.

3 Why do you think the Muslim Sultan of Egypt described his country as an 'earthly paradise' in Source 12?

4 What does Source 12 tell you about his country and its treatment of foreigners?

Islamic government

When Muhammad died, he left no clear instructions as to who should follow him as leader of the Muslim community. The Muslims in Mecca and Medina knew that no one could replace Muhammad as God's messenger, but they still needed someone to guide them. Muhammad's companions chose Abu Bakr, one of his closest friends, to be their leader.

The first caliph

The Muslims gave Abu Bakr the title of 'khalifa' (in English, CALIPH). This Arabic word means 'deputy' or 'successor'. It was Abu Bakr's duty to do everything Muhammad had done for his people (except of course to bring messages from God). As caliph, Abu Bakr was guardian of the new Islamic territories, and defender of the Muslim faith. He had responsibility as:

- ruler of the people
- chief judge
- commander of the army
- leader of public prayers and sometimes preacher in the mosque.

Abu Bakr ruled well and was succeeded by three other caliphs – Umar, Uthman and Ali (who was Muhammad's son in law – see Source 14). Together these first four Muslim rulers are known as 'the rightly guided caliphs', since they had all known Muhammad, and had listened to his teaching. They led the Muslim people faithfully and well.

SOURCE 14
Ali, Muhammad's son-in-law, preaching to a group of his followers.

> Obey God and obey the Prophet and those of you who hold authority.

SOURCE 15
From the Qur'an (4:59).

> Oh my servants . . . do not oppress one another.

SOURCE 16
A hadith or saying of the Prophet Muhammad.

'Abu Bakr prayed and gave thanks to God, and then said, 'O people, I have been appointed to rule over you . . . If I do well, help me, and if I do ill, correct me. Truth is loyalty and falsehood is treachery . . . Obey me as long as I obey God and His prophet. And if I disobey God and His prophet, you do not owe me obedience. Come to prayer, and may God have mercy on you.'

SOURCE 13
Part of a speech made by Abu Bakr, when he came to power as the first caliph to rule after Muhammad's death.

ACTIVITY

Work in pairs on this activity. You are Muslim subjects of Abu Bakr who feel badly treated. You decide to complain to the caliph. Use the sources on this page and the sources about Muhammad's teaching in unit 1 to decide what to say.

> When you judge between people, exercise your judgement justly. Excellent is what God exhorts you to do. God hears and perceives all.
>
> God has promised those of you who have believed and done good deeds that He will surely make them come to power in the world just as he vested power in their predecessors, and that He will certainly establish their religion on their behalf.

exhorts: commands and encourages
perceives: sees and understands
vested: given
predecessors: people who lived in earlier times

SOURCE 17
From the Qur'an (4:58 and 24.55).

'In Islam, the government and people are like the tent, the pole and the pegs. The tent is Islam, the pole is the government, the ropes and pegs are the people. None will do without the other.'

SOURCE 18
From an Arabic collection of sayings about government made during the 7th to 9th centuries.

SOURCE 19
A 14th century Egyptian manuscript illustration of a Muslim ruler at his court.

Later caliphs

In later centuries, the caliphs did not all rule as justly or as effectively as the first Muslim leaders. Some caliphs were weak or foolish. Some were pleasure-seekers, who neglected their duties and mistreated their subjects. For many years there were several rulers who claimed the title of caliph. They governed separate parts of the Muslim world, and sometimes fought among themselves.

1 Read Source 17. What effect do you think this passage from the Qur'an might have had on Muslim rulers' behaviour?

2 Do you think this might also refer to ordinary people? In what ways?

Sunnis and Shi'ites

A major division within the Muslim community occurred after 661, when followers of Caliph Ali broke away. They disagreed with the other Muslims over who was to become caliph after Ali's death. They felt that the best ruler would be one of Caliph Ali's young sons, since he was descended from the Prophet Muhammad.

The followers of Caliph Ali's son became known as SHI'ITES (from the Arabic word 'shi'a' which means 'group' or 'party'). Over the years, they chose a number of different people to lead them instead of the caliphs. They also developed their own views about the best way to live as faithful Muslims.

The Shi'ites still exist today as a group within Islam. They make up about 20 per cent of the world population of Muslims. SUNNI Muslims make up the majority group within Islam. Their name comes from the 'sunnah', or example, set by the Prophet Muhammad, which all Muslims try to follow.

Life under Muslim rule

The earliest caliphs ruled from Arabia. Understandably they usually appointed other Arabians to help them govern the fast-growing area under Muslim control. They all shared a common language and way of doing things.

This soon changed. Able people from all the different Muslim lands were employed as advisers, administrators, generals and judges. The best of them performed their duties very well. It is most likely that they would have shared Caliph Abd al-Malik's view of good government (see Source 20). Local rulers who were sympathetic to Islam were also kept on as governors of distant provinces.

SOURCE 22
A 12th century manuscript illustration, showing Muslim farmers at work.

'The son of Caliph Abd al-Malik asked his father, 'What is good government?' The Caliph answered, 'To win the respect and love of the upper classes; to inspire loyalty among the ordinary people by justice and fairness; and to be patient with the mistakes of people who carry out your orders.'

SOURCE 20
From an Arabic collection of sayings about government during the 7th to 9th centuries.

'It is now time to pay the troops and their families, and for the army to set off on campaign, God willing. When this letter reaches you, let me have whatever tax is due from your lands, and send whatever you have collected from your district . . . Don't let me hear that you have delayed sending the tax . . . God will help the people of your land to pay what they owe to the Commander of the Faithful (the Caliph).'

SOURCE 23
A poll tax demand sent by one of the Caliph's officials to a village headman in 710. Only non-Muslims had to pay the tax.

Muslims and non-Muslims

The caliphs and their officials did not try to force anyone to become a Muslim. It was forbidden in the Qur'an (see Source 21). But Muslims had certain advantages, including freedom from paying poll tax. This was collected every year from all non-Muslims and used to support the army and the government.

There is no place for compulsion in religion.

SOURCE 21
From the Qur'an (2:256). This taught Muslims to be tolerant of other religions.

1 Read Source 23. Why is the official anxious to receive the poll tax payment?

2 Do you think the fact that Muslims did not have to pay the poll tax would encourage non-Muslims to convert to Islam?

3 Use the sources on these pages to make a survey about life under Muslim government.

4 Read Source 20 again. Does the British government today have the same aim as Caliph Abd al-Malik?

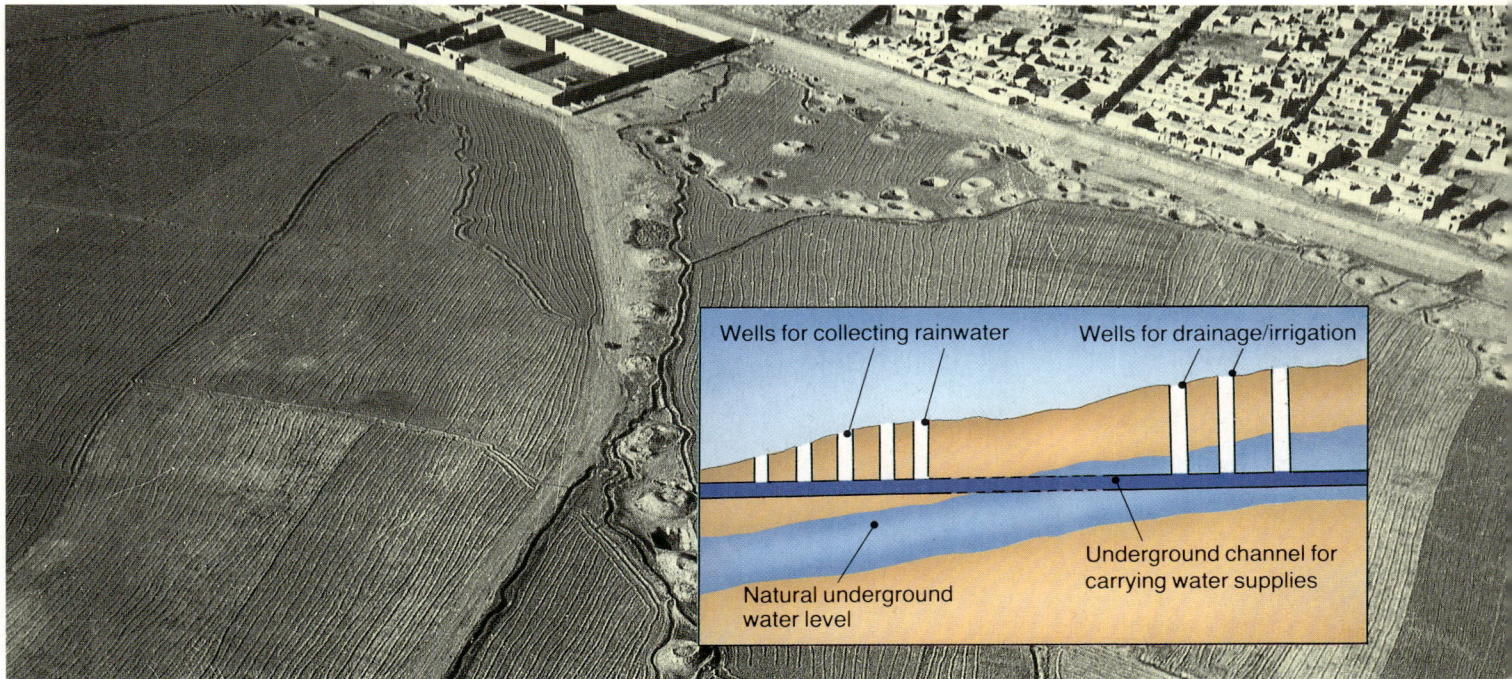

Wells for collecting rainwater   Wells for drainage/irrigation

Underground channel for carrying water supplies

Natural underground water level

Public services

Everybody living in Muslim lands benefited from the results of good government. These included:

- improved roads and bridges
- new IRRIGATION systems (see Source 24)
- defence of borders
- cleaning of streets and markets
- law and order.

Muslims also made regular payments to charity, as Muhammad had taught them. Some of this money was used to help poor Muslims. The rest of it provided services, such as supplies of fresh water or public bath houses which could be used by everyone.

Religion and the law

Muslims and non-Muslims were all governed by the same system of law. Arguments were settled by learned judges called QADIS (see Source 25). They administered Islamic law (called SHAR'IAH) which is based on the teachings of the Qur'an. Shar'iah was introduced in all the lands governed by the Muslims. It replaced many different types of law with a single system.

SOURCE 24
This underground well system is called a QANAT. They were first developed in Muslim lands and are still used in dry areas to provide water from deep underground.

SOURCE 25
This qadi is listening to a family dispute, before making a judgement, based on the teachings of the Qur'an. If a case like this ended in a divorce, the wife returned to her family, with all her possessions.

People of the Book

Islam teaches that there is only one God, who made heaven and earth. Muslims believe that Jews and Christians also worship this God, although, unlike Christians, they do not believe that Jesus Christ was God's son. The city of Jerusalem is sacred to all three religions (see Source 26).

Like Muslims, Jews and Christians have holy scriptures (the Torah and the Bible) which contain rules for living a good life passed down from God. They are therefore also entitled to be called 'People of the Book'.

'Jews and Christians . . . will enjoy protection and care . . . Whoever among them wishes to enter the religion of Islam by the choice of his own heart and by the grace of God . . . may do so and he will be both welcome and blessed. Whoever prefers to keep to his own religion has protection and safeguard . . . and it is the duty of all members of the Muslim community to guard and protect him.'

SOURCE 27
Law announced by the Caliph al-Zahir, who ruled in Egypt during the 11th century.

SOURCE 26
The great mosque in Jerusalem, known as 'The Dome of the Rock'. This site was originally occupied by King Solomon's Temple, a holy place for Jews. The temple was destroyed by Roman soldiers, and a Christian church was built on the site. During the 7th century the caliphs of Baghdad replaced the church with this mosque.

SOURCE 28
Muslim authorities made these rules for Jews and Christians living in 7th century Syria.

- Do not build any new churches or repair old ones.
- Do not give shelter to enemies of the Muslims, or to enemy spies.
- Do not try to stop anyone from becoming a Muslim, or seek to convert anyone to your own faith.
- Show respect to the Muslims.
- Do not wear Muslim clothes; instead, wear something usually a wide belt, or a brightly coloured hood that will mark you out as a non-Muslim.
- Do not carry weapons or ride horses with saddles.
- Do not sell intoxicating drinks.
- Do not build houses overlooking Muslim houses.
- Do not sing loudly in church, or cry noisily during funeral processions.
- Bury your dead away from Muslim graves.
- Do not buy slaves or captives from the wars that belong to the Muslims.
- Anyone who attacks a Muslim will no longer be protected.

Islam teaches that over the centuries, many errors had crept into the Jewish and Christian religions. The early Muslims therefore believed that Jews and Christians were sincere, but misguided. Source 27 shows one Muslim ruler's attitude towards Jews and Christians who lived in his land.

Rules and regulations

Jews and Christians living in Muslim lands usually had to obey special rules drawn up by the local governor (see Sources 28 and 29). These rules also described the kind of protection offered by the government. If they were broken, protection was withdrawn.

These rules may seem harsh to us today, but for the time, they were generous. By comparison, Jews living in Christian Europe were often treated much worse. For example, at the end of the 13th century, King Edward I of England cruelly drove all the Jews out of his kingdom and seized their property.

SOURCE 30
This bowl was made during the 12th century in Egypt by a Muslim craftsman. It shows a Christian priest with an incense burner.

SOURCE 31
Scholars writing in three separate languages at the court of Sicily during the 12th century.

'A Muslim must not massage a Jew or a Christian, (massage to ease away aches and pains was offered at the public baths), nor collect his rubbish nor clean his lavatories . . . A Muslim should not look after the animal belonging to any Jew or Christian, nor serve him as a mule-driver, or as a groom . . .'

SOURCE 29
Regulations made by officials in charge of the markets and other public buildings in Seville, Spain, during the 12th century.

attainment target 1

1 What different attitudes are shown by Muslims towards non-Muslims in Sources 27 to 30?

2 Why do you think these differences existed?

3 Why do you think Muslim governments made special rules for Jews and Christians?

4 What effects do you think the rules in Sources 28 and 29 had on people's everyday lives in a Muslim city with a mixed population?

Friendship and co-operation

In spite of these restrictions, Jews, Christian and Muslims lived and worked peacefully alongside each other in many cities of the Islamic world. They exchanged opinions and ideas, and learned a great deal from one another (see for example Sources 30 and 31). Many Arabic and Islamic words, pastimes, inventions and discoveries were brought to Europe as a result of this friendly co-operation.

Life in Muslim Spain

Spain became part of the Islamic world at the beginning of the 8th century. Muslim rulers built their palaces in the city of Cordoba where they lived until the 13th century. Muslims of several different nationalities settled in Spain during this period. Although many local people converted to Islam, the Muslim rulers allowed Christians and Jews to worship according to their own traditions.

The sources on these two pages show how people of different faiths and nationalities worked, relaxed and studied together, and how life in Muslim Spain was regarded elsewhere in Europe.

SOURCE 32

The Christian cathedral of St Vincent in Cordoba. Christians were allowed to worship here although they were forbidden to disturb the Muslims by the noise of their prayers, or by ringing the bells.

'Who among you studies the Gospels, the Prophets, or the Apostles (or parts of the Bible)? All the young Christians noted for their gifts know only the language and literature of the Arabs, eagerly read and study Arabic books, building up great libraries at enormous cost and loudly proclaiming everywhere that this literature is worthy of admiration. Among thousands of us there is hardly one who can write a Latin letter to a friend, but it is impossible to count the number who can speak and write in Arabic and compose poetry in that language with greater art than the Arabs themselves.'

SOURCE 33

Many Christians studied alongside Muslim scholars. In 854, Alvaro of Cordoba, a Christian, complained that these students were forgetting their own religion and culture.

SOURCE 34

Panel from a carved ivory casket made in Cordoba in 986 for one of the Caliph's sons.
Wealthy Christians and Jews joined Arab noblemen on outings like these.

SOURCE 35

Inside the Great Mosque at Cordoba. Skilled Christian craftsmen, trained in Constantinople, made beautiful mosaic panels for the walls of the mosque. They worked together with Muslims to decorate the interior with the rich colours and designs you can see here.

SOURCE 37

Cordoba was famous throughout Europe. This is what a 10th century nun called Hrosvitha wrote from thousands of kilometres away in Germany.

'Cordoba (is) the jewel of the world – a city well-cultured, rich . . . famous for its charms and well-known for all resources, especially abounding in knowledge.'

Scientific works in Arabic:

Author	Subject
Avicenna (980–1037)	medicine
Rhazes (died c.924)	chemistry, medicine
Averroës (1126–98)	philosophy, medicine

Greek works in Arabic translations:

Author	Subject
Aristotle	physics, natural history
Euclid	mathematics, physics
Archimedes	mathematics
Galen	medicine
Ptolemy	astronomy

SOURCE 36

In Muslim Spain, many important books on scientific subjects were written in Arabic by Muslim and Jewish authors, or were translated into Arabic from ancient Greek texts.

1 Give examples of fact and opinion in Source 33.

2 What does Source 36 tell us about scientific knowledge in Muslim Spain? How important was this for the rest of Europe?

3 Look at Source 37. Hrosvitha spent her life in a German convent. How do you think that she knew about Cordoba? How reliable do you think her comments are?

ACTIVITY

Discuss what you think people in Britain in the 1990s could learn from life in medieval Cordoba.

Two great cities

Rule of the caliphs

In the years following the death of the Prophet Muhammad in 632, more and more land was brought under Muslim control. By 732, the caliphs ruled a vast country, stretching from Spain to India and Central Asia. Source 1 shows the Muslim cities which were important centres of travel and government over the next 500 years.

Merchants and craftsmen from many lands now found it easier to do business with one another, for the following reasons:

- there were internationally agreed laws, based on the teachings of Islam.

- there was an internationally acceptable currency (gold or silver coins) made for the caliphs. Source 2 shows an example.

- best of all, there was an internationally understood language (Arabic), which could be used by SCRIBES from many different lands to record business deals and keep accounts.

AIMS

In this unit, we will look at evidence surviving from Damascus and Baghdad, two great Muslim cities which prospered from the 7th to 13th centuries. What was life like for the people who lived there, and for the caliphs who governed them?

SOURCE 1

Main cities and trade routes in the medieval Muslim world.

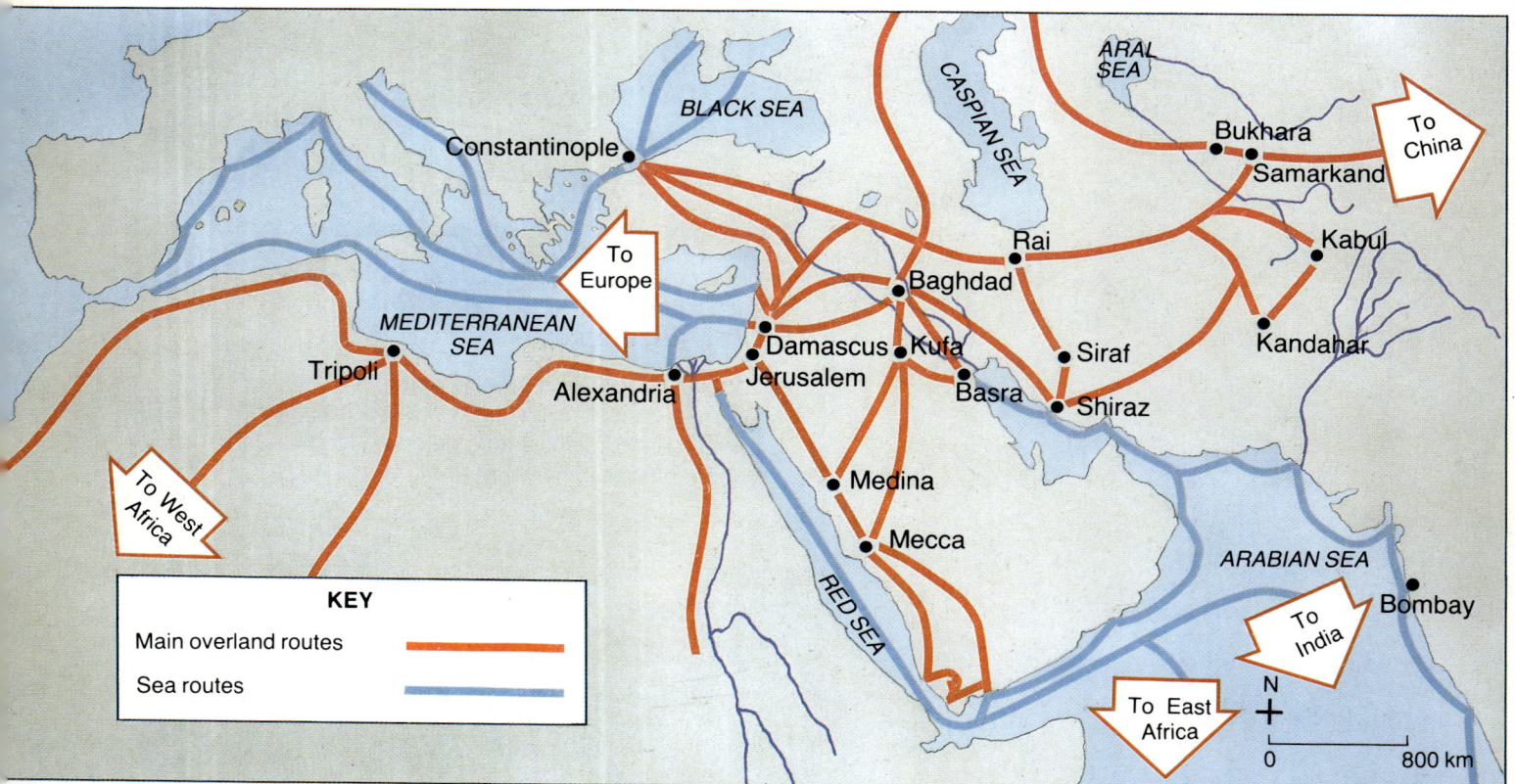

KEY

Main overland routes

Sea routes

Town life

Increased trade brought wealth to merchants and manufacturers, and encouraged the growth of towns (see Sources 3 and 4). Rich people built themselves grand houses and palaces. The remains of these buildings still give us an idea of their splendours. For the poor, home was a simple hut, with a rush mat for sleeping on and a few pots for water and for cooking. Almost nothing has survived of these fragile buildings.

Visitors to a large Muslim town would find streets lined with houses, wells and drinking fountains with fresh running water. There were lively markets and shops bursting with food and all kinds of other goods for sale. In place of desert peace, there was noise and bustle. When this grew unbearable, they could stroll in the orchards and gardens that surrounded the towns, or take a walk along the river bank.

SOURCE 2
Each caliph ordered new coins to be struck when he came to power. This silver coin is decorated with a portrait of Caliph al-Mutawakkil, who ruled from 847 to 861.

SOURCE 3
Although the city of Damascus has grown and changed since the days of the caliphs, you can still see the remains of the old town, with narrow, crowded streets clustered round the Great Mosque.

SOURCE 4
This 15th century picture shows workers using scaffolding to construct the front of a large building. Bricks and mortar are being prepared in the foreground. Similar methods were used in Baghdad and other Middle Eastern cities.

SOURCE 5
The Great Mosque of Damascus,
built by the Umayyads.

SOURCE 6
These mosaics from the Great Mosque in Damascus
show the town houses built when the caliphs ruled.

Caliphs at Damascus

In 661, Ali, the fourth caliph, was murdered by a
religious group who disagreed with his views.
Straight away, Mu'awiya, governor of Syria,
seized control of all the Muslim lands, and
declared himself caliph in Ali's place. The three
earliest caliphs had based their government at
the holy city of Medina in Arabia, but Mu'awiya
wanted to stay in Syria. He was well known
there and he had troops and advisers he could
trust.

As caliph, Mu'awiya was extremely powerful.
Military leaders, lawyers, scholars, government
officials, and all kinds of people sought his help
or protection. They flocked to his court at
Damascus, the largest town in Syria. Merchants,
traders and craftsmen soon followed to sell their
goods to wealthy courtiers and officials. The
quiet town developed rapidly into a busy city
with government buildings, mosques, libraries,
houses, shops, public baths, hostels for travellers
and, of course, a magnificent palace for the caliph
himself.

Mu'awiya and his successors stayed in power in
Damascus for almost a hundred years. (They
were all members of the rich and powerful
Umayyad family, and so historians call them the
Umayyad caliphs.) But in 750, they were
overthrown by a new ruling family, known as
the Abbasids. The Abbasid caliphs were ruthless.
They hunted down and killed all the members of
the Umayyad family they could find. Only a few
managed to escape. In this way, the Abbasids
strengthened their control over Muslim lands.

'Do not stay in a country which lacks these five
things: a strong government, a just judge, a secure
market, a wise physician, a flowing river.'

SOURCE 7
Arab saying, from a collection
made in the 9th century.

Baghdad, a new city

The Abbasids defeated the Umayyads because they had powerful allies, particularly in countries to the east of Syria. In addition many people were unhappy with the way in which the Umayyad caliphs had ruled. They accused them of being selfish and greedy.

For these reasons, the Abbasids decided that it would be safer to build themselves an entirely new city, close to the lands where they had allies. They chose a site in Iraq, occupied by a small village called Baghdad. It was in the centre of a fertile plain, well supplied with water, and close to several major trade routes. Caliph al-Mansur, who founded the city, claimed that it would be 'a market place for the world'. He was so excited when he first saw the site that he exclaimed, 'Praise be to God who preserved it for me, and caused all those who came before me to neglect it.'

Caliph al-Mansur proved to be a good judge when it came to choosing a site for a city. Baghdad soon grew to be larger and more prosperous than Damascus had ever been. It remained one of the most important trading cities in the Muslim world for over 300 years.

'I mention Baghdad first because it is . . . the greatest city, which has no equal in the east or west of the world in extent, size, prosperity, abundance of water, or health of climate, and because it is inhabited by all kinds of people, town-dwellers and country-dwellers. To it they come from all countries, far and near, and people from every side have preferred Baghdad to their own homelands . . .

. . . the character of the inhabitants is good, their faces bright and their minds untrammelled (unworried). The people excel in knowledge, understanding, letters, manners, insight . . . skill in commerce and crafts, cleverness in every argument, proficiency in every calling (trade or occupation), and mastery of every craft.'

SOURCE 8
This description was written in the 9th century, by a proud citizen of Baghdad.

1 Study Sources 6, 8 and 9. What is the value of each type of source for the historian seeking to find out about past cities?

2 Source 8 is a mixture of information and opinion. Read it carefully, and find two examples of factual information (which could be proved right from other sources), and one example of the writer's opinions.

SOURCE 9
The city of Baghdad, before its destruction in 1258.

SOURCE 10
Standard bearers from the caliph's army. A 13th century manuscript illustration from Baghdad.

SOURCE 12
Remains of an 8th century desert palace in present-day Jordan.

The royal household

The Abbasid caliphs were enormously wealthy. Their riches came from two sources: taxes and trade. Some of this money went to pay the salaries of government officials, or in wages, food and lodgings for the vast staff that was needed to run the caliph's household. The staff included cooks, nurserymaids, musicians and gardeners. Some money was spent on feeding and equipping the caliph's personal bodyguards and on the army which was kept ready to defend the Muslim lands from attack.

The caliphs spent lavishly on new buildings, sumptuous furnishings, beautiful mosques, and on wonderful clothes and jewels for themselves, their wives and their companions. Source 14 lists some of these possessions.

'In the centre of the great square stood the palace, the entrance of which was called the Golden Gate, and next to it was the principal mosque. All around the palace was no building or private house, or dwelling, except for a building on the side of the Syria Gate for the horse guards and a great long gallery supported on columns of kiln-burnt bricks and plaster. The chief of police sat in the one, the commander of the guard in another . . .

All around the square were the dwellings of the young sons of al-Mansur, the black slaves who served him, the treasury, the arsenal (where weapons were stored), the chancery (where lawyers worked), the office of the land-tax, the office of the seal (where documents were authorised), the office of the army, the office of supplies, the office of the palace staff, the public kitchens, and the office of expenditure.'

SOURCE 11
A description of the palace built by al-Mansur, the founder of Baghdad, between 663 and 675. The buildings were finished about ten years before Harun al-Rashid came to power.

The caliphs also bought presents for other rulers whom they wanted to befriend. For example, Caliph Harun al-Rashid sent a live elephant, a silken robe, jewels, scent, ivory and a clever water-powered clock to King Charlemagne of France. He hoped to negotiate a peace treaty with Charlemagne.

At Damascus and Baghdad, the caliphs built palaces at the centre of their cities. Here they lived in luxury, entertained important guests and stored their documents, treasures and weapons.

SOURCE 13
This manuscript illustration shows Caliph al-Mamun (813 – 33) taking a shower, having a haircut, and receiving a relaxing massage in the splendid bath-house attached to his palace in Baghdad.

SOURCE 14
Some of the possessions of Caliph Harun al-Rashid at the time of his death in 809.

This list was compiled by one of palace treasurers, who reported that it took him four months to count all the caliph's belongings. As well as these moveable goods, the caliph also owned vast amounts of land and hundreds of buildings.

4,000 embroidered robes
4,000 silk cloaks lined with furs
10,000 shirts and shifts
10,000 caftans
2,000 pairs of trousers
4,000 turbans
1,000 capes
1,000 precious china vessels

Many kinds of perfume
Jewels valued by jewellers at 4 million dinars

500,000 dinars (in cash)
1,000 jewelled rings

1,000 Armenian carpets
4,000 curtains
5,000 cushions
5,000 pillows
1,500 silk carpets
100 silk rugs
1,000 silk cushions and pillows
1,000 Darabjirdi carpets (ie from Darabjir)
1,000 silk cushions
1,000 silk curtains
300 Tabari carpets (ie from Tabar)
1,000 washbasins
300 stoves
1,000 candlesticks
1,000 belts
10,000 decorated swords
50,000 swords for the guards and pages
150,000 lances
100,000 bows

1,000 special suits of armour
50,000 common suits of armour
10,000 helmets
20,000 breastplates
150,000 shields
4,000 special saddles
30,000 common saddles
4,000 pairs of half (short) boots, most of them lined with sable, mink and other kinds of fur, with a knife and a kerchief in each boot
4,000 pairs of socks
4,000 small tents with their fittings

brocade: a richly-patterned fabric
caftan: a loose, flowing robe
dinars: solid gold or silver coins

ACTIVITY

Caliph Harun al-Rashid's palace was destroyed, by invading Mongol armies in 1258. But we can find out what it was like by using a number of different types of evidence:

- documents
- manuscript illustrations
- ruined buildings
- remains discovered by ARCHAEOLOGISTS
- pictures of similar buildings on coins, mosaics, etc.

Not all this evidence is of equal value. Some is incomplete. Some can only tell us what the palace *might* have looked like. Other evidence can give us first-hand information about the palace and how it was constructed.

Look at Sources 5 to 13. Use them to help you 'reconstruct' the Caliph's palace at the height of its glory, before it was destroyed.

1 First, make a table like this one, to help you judge the value of the different sources. Fill it in with your decisions about each source:

Source	Amount of information about the Caliph's palace at Baghdad		
	Nothing	Incomplete	A good deal

Source	Accuracy of information about the Caliph's palace at Baghdad			
	Unlikely to be true	Tells us what palace might have looked like	Eyewitness	Likely to be true

2 a What would you want to know about Source 8 in order to decide how reliable it is?

 b Compare Source 5 (a mosaic detail) with Source

 c Source 14 is a list of possessions. What can it tell us about the palace, the building and its furnishings?

3 Now, work with a partner to compile a 'reconstruction' of the palace, One of you should make a list of things we know for certain about the palace and its contents, the other one should make a list of things that might have been there.

What we know for certain was there	Source number

What we think might have been there	Source number

4 From the same sources, work out what you can about Caliph Harun al-Rashid's clothes and jewels, his palace bodyguards, and the furnishings in his palace.

5 Imagine you are a visitor to the Caliph's court. Write a letter home, describing your first glimpse of the Caliph and his surroundings.

SOURCE 15
This 12th century manuscript illustration shows wealthy citizens enjoying entertainment in a pleasant Baghdad garden.

> Oh God, my whole occupation and all my desire in the world . . . is to remember Thee; and in the world to come, of all things my desire is to meet Thee . . .

SOURCE 16
Part of a prayer written by Rabi'ah al-Adawiyyah.

'She had the deepest desire to do good. She was the swiftest to perform pious deeds, and the readiest to give to the poor. Among her other good works, she brought water to the sanctuary at Mecca after the supply had failed.'

SOURCE 17
A description of Zubaidah, written by a 9th century historian.

Caliphs and their cities

The extravagant and selfish lives led by many of the Abbasid caliphs and their palace companions were strongly criticised by some individuals. Many Muslims felt that their rulers did not set a good example to the people. They ignored their duties in government and as leading Muslims.

Source 15 shows a wealthy group of men being entertained by a musician and storyteller. It must have been a great temptation for the caliphs to spend their time pleasantly like this, rather than carrying out their duties as rulers. Some caliphs simply relied on officials and generals to run the government for them.

Two Muslim women

Although women played no part in public life, they managed to make their opinions felt, even when they criticised those in power. Rabi'ah al-Adawiyyah, for example, was a remarkable woman who lived during the 8th century in Basra, a city under the rule of the Baghdad caliphs. She chose to follow a life of prayer and poverty because she wanted to remind people of their duty towards God, and encourage them to live as faithful Muslims (see Source 16). Like many other Muslim thinkers at the time, she criticised the extravagance of the caliphs and their courtiers. Many men and women listened to what Rabi'ah had to say, and tried to follow her example.

Women who lived at the caliph's court led very different lives from Rabi'ah. Source 17 describes Zubaidah, the wife of Harun al-Rashid, who was surrounded by the glamour and politics of palace life. She is remembered today for her gifts to charity, especially for building guest houses and wells along the pilgrim routes to Mecca. There, weary travellers, both rich and poor, could find rest and refreshment. Zubaidah made six pilgrimages to Mecca in all, and completed her building project on the final one.

Why do you think people listened to Rabi'ah's criticisms of the caliphs? Was it because she was a woman, because she was poor or because she lived a holy life and spoke to people about their religious duties?

A trading city

Baghdad was situated close to some of the most important international trade routes, leading from China to the countries bordering the Mediterranean Sea. Ships laden with goods from India and the islands of the East Indies sailed up the River Tigris to supply the city's markets. Camel caravans arrived overland with rare and beautiful objects from Central Asia and China, and from the lands bordering the Mediterranean Sea.

The sources on this page show what city markets were like. Craftsmen and dealers in particular goods were grouped together in a particular SOUK (market), so it was easy to compare prices for similar items.

Left-over and rotten fish should not be sold.

The furriers must be advised not to use pigeons' dung to disguise worn-out furs. This is a deceit which they practise.

Fruit must not be sold before it is ripe, for this is bad . . .

SOURCE 18
Some examples of market regulations from the 13th century.

SOURCE 20
This crystal bottle is another example of Muslim workmanship. It was traded to Constantinople and later looted by Crusader troops.

SOURCE 19
This beautiful coronation robe was made by Muslim craftsmen for King Roger of Sicily in the 12th century. Skilfully embroidered silks and brocades were also on sale in the markets of the Middle East.

Market rules

The caliphs' officials were clever merchants. They bought and sold goods to make a profit for their masters. They also collected rents and TOLLS from all the market traders. Like the taxes from the provinces, this money went to make the caliphs rich.

Government officials drew up rules and regulations to make sure that market traders dealt fairly with their customers. Source 18 shows some examples of these rules from another Muslim country, Spain.

SOURCE 21
Eleventh century illustration of a slave market.

The slave market

As you will see from Sources 21 and 22, trading activities included buying and selling slaves. Slaves worked in the households of rich people and helped to build some of the city's grand buildings. Slavery is a practice that we do not find acceptable today, but during the Middle Ages it was widespread throughout the Middle East, Asia and in the Christian countries of southern Europe. Islam taught that Muslims should not enslave fellow Muslims, so Arabian traders purchased slaves from local dealers in more distant lands.

Islam encouraged people who bought slaves to care for them properly, especially when they were old or ill. Some slaves lived comfortably. Sadly, others were badly treated by their owners.

Imagine that you are a wealthy citizen of Baghdad who has just built a new house in the city. Make a list of the items you would buy to furnish your new home.

SOURCE 22
From a 9th century manuscript called 'A Clear Look at Trade', which described the various goods on sale in the great market centres such as Baghdad.

From India: tigers, leopards, elephants, leopard skins, red rubies, ebony, coconuts . . .

From China: silk, porcelain, paper, ink, peacocks, fiery horses, saddles, felt, cinnamon, rhubarb . . .

From the Byzantines: silver and gold vessels, pure imperial dinars, embroidered cloths, brocades, fiery horses, slave girls, red copper articles, strong locks, lyres, marble workers, specialists in cultivation . . .

From Arabia: Arab horses, ostriches, thoroughbred she-camels, tanned hides . . .

From North Africa: leopards, felt, black falcons . . .

From Egypt: ambling donkeys, fine cloths, papyrus, balsam oil, high grade topaz . . .

From the Khazars (present-day southern Russia): slaves, armour, helmets, hoods of mail . . .

From Balkh and its region (in present-day Afghanistan): good grapes and mushrooms . . .

From Isfahan (in present-day Iran): honeycombs, quinces, Chinese pears, apples, salt, saffron, potash, white lead, bunk beds in tiers, fine cloths, fruit drinks . . .

SOURCE 23
A 13th century bowl from Persia, showing people riding an Indian elephant.

Retreat to Samarra

During the 9th century, the caliphs built a completely new palace city for themselves at Samarra, about 120 kilometres to the north of Baghdad (see Source 24). Here they could live safely, and house their armies of slaves and freedmen. They could also escape the criticism caused by their extravagant lifestyle.

The building of Samarra was the greatest project undertaken by the caliphs after the construction of Baghdad itself. The huge complex was completed in only 46 years. However, the cost was high: when Caliph al-Mutadid came to power in 892, he found that the palace treasury was empty. He left Samarra and returned to live in Baghdad. From that point the beautiful palace city began to decline, and was never again restored.

The ruins of Samarra. The main palace and other buildings for staff and courtiers stretched 35 kilometres along the banks of the River Tigris. The whole area was surrounded by a strong wall and guarded by soldiers.

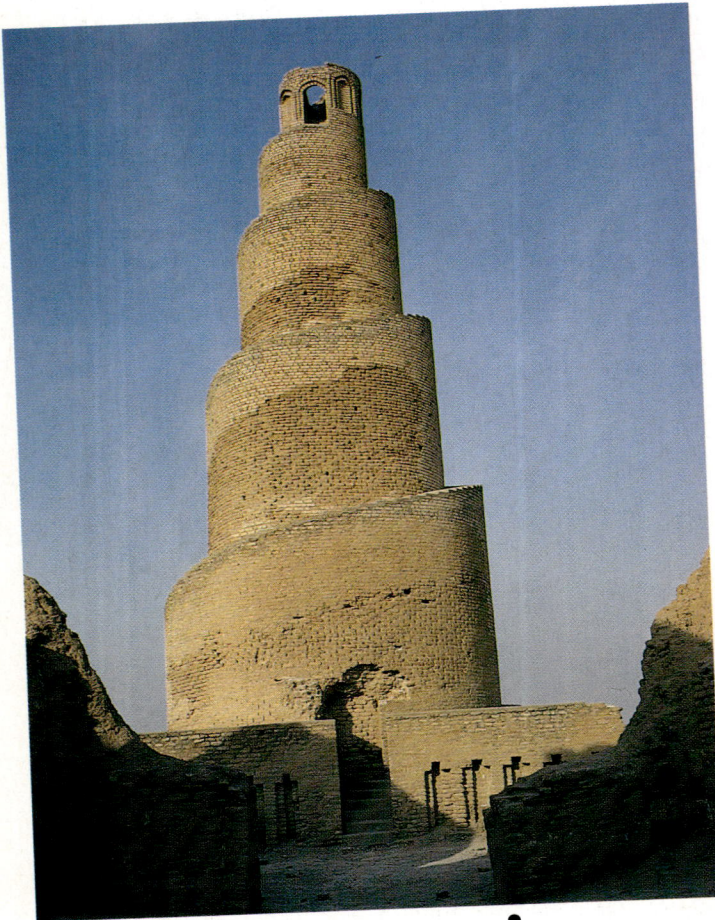

SOURCE 25
Remains of the mosque tower at Samarra.

Palace politics

After the death of Caliph Harun al-Rashid in 809, there were violent struggles between rivals, each claiming the right to be the next caliph. Throughout the 9th century there were plots, murders, attempted revolutions, betrayals and slave revolts.

Security for the caliph became all-important. The later Abbasid caliphs spent an increasing amount of their money on private armies of specially trained foreign slaves to act as bodyguards. These armies were feared and hated by the ordinary citizens of Baghdad.

The Abbasid caliphs themselves were no longer regarded as good 'Commanders of the Faithful', but criticised and mocked like any other ruler who was slowly losing power. Stories were told about their extravagance, their cruelty, and poor government.

Sources 26 and 27 show how courtiers tried to win favour from the caliphs. Successful rulers like Harun al-Rashid knew how to control crafty courtiers, but in later years the caliph's palace was often seething with plots, rumours and corruption.

The end of the Abbasids

If the caliph could not control his own courtiers and officials, how could he continue to rule the rest of his lands? All too often, he could not. During the 9th and 10th centuries, other Muslim rulers in far-flung territories became increasingly powerful, until they were strong enough to disobey the caliph's commands if they chose to. Gradually they broke away to form separate states. Baghdad was no longer a great capital city, but just one big market centre among many others.

attainment target 3

1 What does Source 26 tell us about Harun al-Rashid?

2 In what way does Source 27 throw doubt on the truth of Source 26?

3 Suggest reasons why the courtier might have written the poem in Source 26.

'You have stretched out the hand of nobility to us, east and west, and bestowed bounty (gifts) on the easterner and westener.

You have adorned (made beautiful) the face of the earth with generosity . . .

O Commander of the Faithful, brave and pious (respectful to God) . . .

God has destined that the kingdom should remain to Harun, and God's destiny is binding on mankind.

The world submits to Harun, the favoured of God . . .'

SOURCE 26
Part of a praise poem written about Caliph Harun al-Rashid by one of his courtiers.

The fall of Baghdad

By the beginning of the 10th century, the Baghdad caliphs no longer held any real power. The Abbasids were replaced by other rulers, and military leaders competed with each other for control of the Muslim lands. In 1055, the Seljuks, another powerful Muslim group, replaced the caliphs as rulers in Baghdad. They were excellent soldiers and under their rule many Muslim territories were governed more effectively.

However, this settled period came to an end, with an invasion from the East. In 1258, Baghdad was attacked by Mongol armies. (You can read more about these fierce invaders on pages 56 and 57.) The Mongols burned most of Baghdad to the ground. The once-glorious city of Caliph Harun al-Rashid was gone for ever.

A powerful Sultan (ruler) was hungry, and so his servants brought him a dish of cooked aubergines. It was delicious.
'Aubergines are very good to eat,' said the Sultan. One of his courtiers immediately began to praise aubergines, repeating over and over again what wonderful vegetables they were. The Sultan grew tired of this and to make him stop talking, said, 'Aubergines can be very bad for you.'
'Of course,' agreed the courtier and started a long speech about how dangerous it was to eat even a small piece of aubergine.
The Sultan was astonished. 'What's all this?' he cried. 'You've only just stopped telling me that aubergines are wonderful.'
'That's right,' agreed the courtier, 'but I'm your courtier. I have to say what pleases you, not what pleases the aubergines.'

SOURCE 27
Stories like this were told by storytellers to entertain the crowds.

attainment target 1

Compare the role of the Abbasid caliphs in Baghdad, described in this unit, with the role of the 'rightly guided caliphs' (see pages 20-21). What differences were there at court, and for the people?

Arts and sciences

Places of worship

In many civilisations, the best buildings and the finest works of art are usually produced for one of two purposes: to praise God or to glorify the ruler. This is true of Islam, although the greatest skill, care and money has been devoted to places of worship.

Beautiful MOSQUES can be found throughout the world, and many ancient Muslim buildings are still in regular use. The wealthy PATRONS who paid for them to be built made sure that only the very best materials were used (see Sources 1 and 2).

Other buildings with a religious purpose included monasteries, colleges (see Source 3), houses of prayer, and tombs.

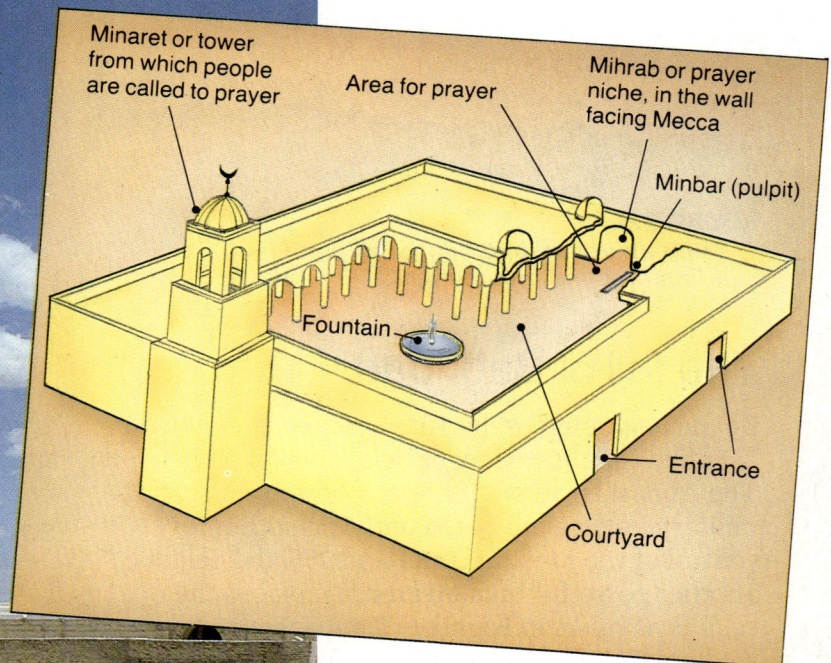

Minaret or tower from which people are called to prayer

Area for prayer

Mihrab or prayer niche, in the wall facing Mecca

Minbar (pulpit)

Fountain

Entrance

Courtyard

SOURCE 1

The Great Mosque at Qayrawan, Tunisia, built in the 9th century. The diagram marks the key features found in mosques throughout the world.

SOURCE 2

This huge wool carpet dates from 1540 and was once used to cover the floor of a mosque in Ardabil, near the Caspian Sea.

SOURCE 3

This MADRASA (college), was built in the early 14th century in Fez, Morocco. It is decorated with patterned mosaics and the upper walls are made of finely carved stone.

> God loves that whenever any of you does anything, he does it in the best way.

SOURCE 4

From a collection of hadith.

Although the style of architecture varied from place to place, all Muslim religious buildings had one thing in common. There were no pictures of people or animals used to decorate them, only abstract designs. Can you remember the reason for this? (See page 9.)

Muslim craftsmen and women produced many wonderful textiles including patterned silk and cloth of gold. High quality carpets were made in Turkey and Central Asia. These furnished palaces and covered the floors where Muslims prayed (see Source 2). Important buildings were lit by oil lamps made of glass or delicately worked metal.

1 What materials have been used in the sources on these pages?

2 What skills are needed to work those materials?

3 In what ways do Sources 1 to 3 support Muhammad's saying in Source 4?

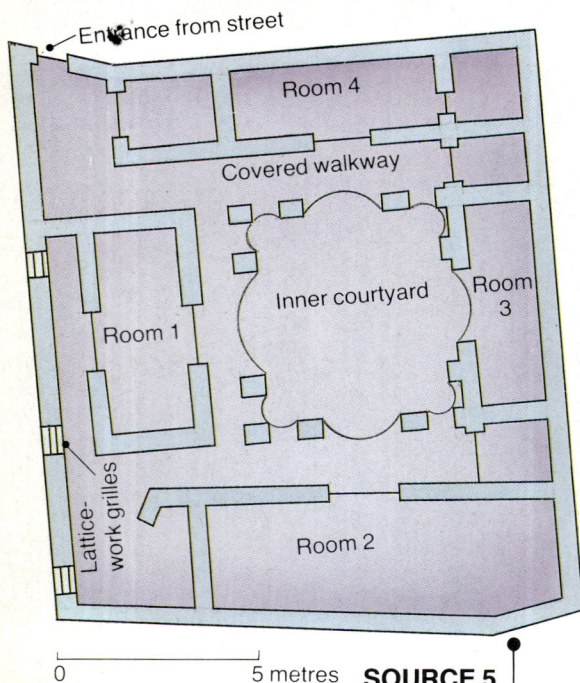

Entrance from street

Room 4

Covered walkway

Room 1

Inner courtyard

Room 3

Lattice-work grilles

Room 2

0 5 metres

SOURCE 5
Plan of a medieval Muslim house in Cordoba, Spain. Houses similar to this were built in many Muslim cities. Many had lavatories and drains, which were almost unknown in Northern Europe at that time.

SOURCE 6
The Court of Lions in the Alhambra Palace, Granada, Spain. The rulers of Granada ordered building to start here in 1248, and the palace took one hundred years to complete.

SOURCE 7
This magnificent water flask was made in Syria during the 13th century. It is made of brass, inlaid with silver.

In the home

Houses were built for comfort and privacy. As you can see from Source 5, rooms were arranged around a central courtyard, with covered walkways where people could shelter from the heat of the day. Orange and lemon trees, and perhaps a vine, grew in tubs in the courtyard, and water trickled from a cooling fountain. Source 5 shows only a ground floor plan, but many houses also had an upper storey, with a balcony looking down into the courtyard.

The outer walls of these town houses were thick and solid, with a securely guarded entrance and only a few windows facing on to the hot, dusty streets. Wealthy families owned large houses with separate courtyards and private rooms for the women of the household. Space was set aside for entertaining and also for work.

People who could afford it decorated their houses with fine wooden doors, elaborate window shutters and carved stonework (see Source 6). Wealthy Muslims paid high prices for skilled workmanship such as that shown in Source 7.

Gardens

Gardens were important in Muslim lands. They provided coolness and shade after the heat and dust of deserts and busy towns (see Source 10).

As you can see in Source 8, people admired the beauty of the plants and the skill of the gardeners. Gardens were special for another reason as well. They reminded everyone that God had promised, in the Qur'an, to provide a wonderful reward after death to Muslims who had lived good and useful lives (see Source 9).

'Nearby are many spacious, sumptuous gardens full of all sorts of fruit trees . . . lemons, limes, oranges, apricots . . . These gardens are watered morning and evening by water drawn from the Nile by cattle and horses.'

SOURCE 8
Report from a French ambassador (around 1510) about the gardens near his lodgings not far from the River Nile in Egypt.

Those who have believed and done righteous deeds, theirs will be the gardens of Paradise, a place to dwell eternally, with never a wish to be away.

SOURCE 9
From the Qur'an (18:107-8). Paradise is described as a beautiful garden.

ACTIVITY

1 With a partner, compare the Muslim house plan in Source 5 with the North European one in Source 11.
   - Make a list of differences.
   - Suggest reasons for these differences.
   - Which would you prefer to live in?

2 From the information given in the sources on these pages, draw a plan of a medieval Muslim town garden. Be sure to include:
   - suitable plants
   - source of water
   - shady walkway.

SOURCE 10
The Generalife fountain and garden, in the Alhambra palace.

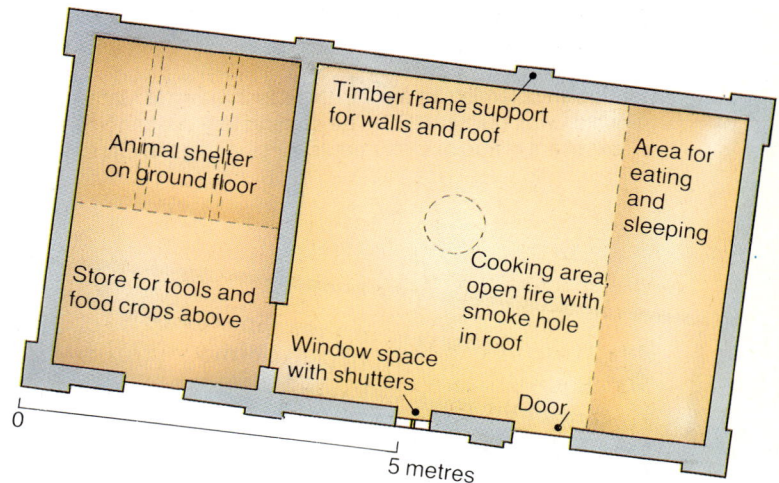

Timber frame support for walls and roof

Animal shelter on ground floor

Area for eating and sleeping

Store for tools and food crops above

Cooking area, open fire with smoke hole in roof

Window space with shutters

Door

0   5 metres

SOURCE 11
Plan of a medieval house in a typical North European village.

SOURCE 12

Muslim scientists at work in the observatory at Maragha, which was built in 1258. The observatory contained an excellent range of instruments for studying the stars.

If anyone travels on a road in search of knowledge, God will cause him to travel on one of the roads in Paradise.

SOURCE 13

From a collection of hadith.

'In the name of God, the Merciful, the Compassionate. May God have mercy on all who ask for his mercy for the humble person who built this blessed place and made it a primary school for the children of Muslims . . . to learn the Qur'an. Money from the fund is to be spent on the schoolmaster . . . the school . . . the lighting of the lamp . . . water for all the children to wash their slates and to drink, on condition that the schoolmaster be a pious and godly man.'

SOURCE 14

Sign outside a school in Jerusalem, 1199.

Islamic education

Islam teaches that learning is important for two reasons:

- to find out more about God and the world he created;

- to discover new knowledge that can improve people's lives.

Education and knowledge were highly valued in the Muslim world (see Sources 12 and 13). Muslim rulers built colleges, libraries and OBSERVATORIES in their capital cities. Wealthy individuals gave money to found schools and to support pupils (see Source 14).

Many Muslim colleges, called MADRASAS, were built during the Middle Ages. Often, they were close to mosques and libraries in the centre of important towns. At the madrasa, students studied the Qur'an and learned to read and write the Arabic language. They could also study SHARI'AH, (Islamic law, based on the Qur'an). Muslim students learned about philosophy, science, mathematics and ASTRONOMY (see Source 12) at universities throughout Asia and the Middle East.

1 What does Source 14 tell you about the reasons for founding this school?

2 What were the children supposed to learn there?

3 How was the school paid for?

4 Why do you think the schoolmaster had to be a 'pious and godly man'?

Medicine

Medicine was one of the most respected branches of learning. Doctors used medicines made from herbs and plants (see Source 15). Their knowledge came from making careful scientific observations of various diseases, and from watching their patients' progress (see Source 16). Chemists who sold medicines had shops and stalls in most big towns. Hospitals, with wards, patients, and a full-time staff of doctors and medical students, were first developed in Muslim cities.

In contrast, some European doctors were still trying to treat their patients by reciting magic charms or by consulting horoscopes. Others, however, learned from Muslim medicine, and greatly improved their standard of medical care.

SOURCE 15
Scene at a chemist's, 13th century. Herbs were collected, stored and used in medical mixtures as shown here.

- The physician does not work the cure. He does but prepare the path for nature, the real healer.

- The better you know and understand the temperament and characteristics of the patient while he is healthy, and the more you feel his pulse and examine his urine, the more easily you will cure him.

- There are illnesses which are healed merely by your preventing the patient from pursuing evil habits . . .

- Reassure and encourage the patient with the prospect of recovery, even if you are not sure of it, for thus you will strengthen his nature.

SOURCE 16
Extracts from a textbook, written in the 9th century by a Jewish doctor working with Muslim patients and students.

Preserving 'lost' knowledge

As well as making investigations and discoveries of their own, Muslim scholars worked with others to translate important Greek and Roman scientific works into Arabic. In this way, valuable knowledge which had been lost or forgotten in Europe was preserved and developed. This knowledge was welcomed by scholars from all nations.

SOURCE 17
This 14th century jar was designed to store herbal medicines.

Muslim adviser at a siege (around 1310). You can see him at the far right of the picture, wearing a turban. The giant catapult in the picture is known as a MANGONEL. It was designed to hurl heavy objects at the city walls and break holes in them.

'The first night I spent in his presence I found a great gathering of scholars who were discussing various sciences. Saladin began to make an outstanding contribution to the discussions. He began to speak of the business of building walls and digging trenches around Jerusalem. He took charge of it himself, and even carried stones on his shoulders, so that everyone, rich and poor, strong and weak, followed his example . . .'

SOURCE 19
Description of a visit to Salah el-Din Yusuf ibn-Ayyub, known in Europe as Saladin, the great Muslim army commander who lived in the 12th century.

Take 10 pounds of tar, 3 pounds of resin, 1.5 pounds each of sandrac and lac, 3 pounds of pure, good quality sulphur . . . 5 pounds of melted dolphin fat, the same quantity of melted fat from goats' kidneys . . .

If you wish to use it in time of war, take a quantity of the above mixture add about a tenth part of mineral sulphur which is greenish and looks like old oil, place the whole in a pan and heat it until it is about to burn . . . Put into an earthenware pot, with a piece of felt. Then throw it with a mangonel against whatever you wish to burn. It will never be extinguished.

SOURCE 20
Part of a 12th century recipe for making naphtha, a fire-bomb which could not be extinguished by water. It required a wide range of exotic ingredients. Making it was also extremely dangerous.

Science and technology

During the Middle Ages, Muslim military machines and inventions were world famous. Muslim scientists and engineers were employed by many non-Muslim kings and princes to train their armies and to act as advisers in battle (see Source 18). Muslim forces used NAPHTHA (a form of explosive – see Source 20) to set fire to buildings and ships during the CRUSADES. European military experts did not discover how to make naphtha until much later.

However, most Muslim technology was put to work for peaceful purposes. Muslim countries were often hot and dry, so water was the key to growing enough food for the people. Muslim engineers developed many machines to help peasants and farmers to irrigate their land and grow better crops.

If you turn back to page 23 you will see how the qanat well system worked. It supplied water to vast areas of land that would otherwise have been semi-desert. Huge water wheels like the ones in Source 21 were also used to channel water to nearby fields.

Counting and measurement

Muslim scientists were world leaders in many areas of discovery. In the 11th century they were the first to make magnifying lenses. They also developed measuring instruments such as the KAMAL and the ASTROLABE shown in Source 22. Both these instruments helped sailors to find out the position of their ship, once they had lost sight of land.

Muslim mathematicians were especially famous. Even the word 'algebra' comes from the Arabic word 'al-jabr', which means 'the binding together of disorganised parts'. As Source 23 shows, they developed a whole new system of numbers, based on Hindu originals, and introduced the concept of zero to the West. This made calculations much easier and helped Muslim scholars to make new mathematical discoveries.

SOURCE 21
Water wheels like these on the Hama River in Syria have been in use since the 12th century.

1 What kind of building technology is Saladin discussing in Source 19?

2 In what ways do you think Muslim interest in mathematics and precision instruments helped them with other achievements in
- water engineering
- architecture
- medicine
- navigation?

Hindu

Arabic

Europe (12th century)

Europe (15th century)

SOURCE 22
A medieval astrolabe. It contains place names from Arabia, India, and south-east Russia.

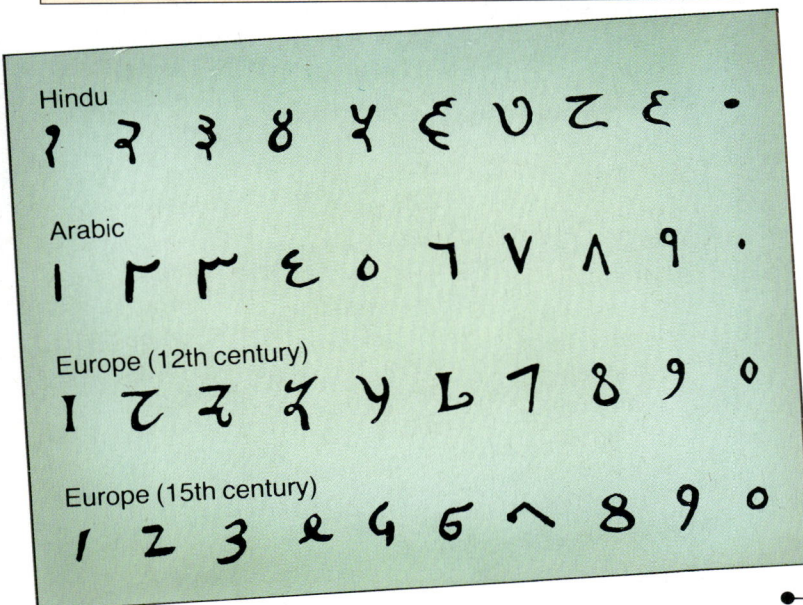

SOURCE 23
This diagram shows how medieval Arabic numerals gradually turned into the numbers we use today.

SOURCE 24
A page from the beautifully illustrated Persian history manuscript, 'The Book of Kings', 13th century.

'A flowering of Islamic culture'

This phrase was used by one modern historian to describe the achievements of Muslim writers and thinkers during the Middle Ages. In addition to works on science and medicine, there were books written on law, history and philosophy. Maps and guides were produced by learned geographers, and Muslim travellers and explorers wrote exciting books about their adventures.

Many of the manuscripts produced by these writers were beautiful objects in themselves, as Source 24 shows. They were also extremely valuable, and were usually carefully stored in libraries (see Source 26).

Source 25 contains an extract from the AUTOBIOGRAPHY (life story) of Avicenna, a brilliant scientist and philosopher who worked as court doctor in a number of royal Muslim households, at the end of the 10th century. His fame spread world-wide, and many Jewish, Christian and Muslim scholars turned to him for advice. He wrote his autobiography towards the end of his life.

'For a year and a half, I devoted myself to study. During this time, I never slept a whole night through and did nothing but study all day long. I acquired great knowledge . . . Whenever I was puzzled by a problem, I would go to the mosque, pray, and beg the Creator of All to reveal that which was hidden from me and make easy that which was difficult. Then at night I would return home, put a lamp in front of me, and set to work reading and writing.

Whenever sleep overcame me or when I felt exhausted, I would drink a modest cup to restore my strength, and then go on reading. When I dozed, I would dream of the same problem, so that for many problems the solution appeared to me in my sleep. I went on like this until I was firmly grounded in all sciences, and had mastered them as far as was humanly possible . . . Then I returned to the study of divine science . . . When I reached the age of eighteen, I had completed the study of all these sciences. At that point my memory was better, whereas today my learning is riper.'

SOURCE 25
In this extract, Avicenna (980–1037) remembers how he spent his days when he was sixteen.

---

attainment target 3

1 Give three words to describe Avicenna's character, as it appears in Source 25.

2 What does Source 25 tell us about his religious beliefs?

3 Look at Sources 3, 13, 14 and 26 in this unit. What do the Sources tell us about the links between religion and education?

4 Which of Sources 3, 13, 14, 25 and 26 is the most useful for finding out about the education of ordinary people in Muslim lands?

5 Select four sources from this unit to show the achievements of Islamic civilisation in
   ● building
   ● technology
   ● science
   ● medicine
   Explain your choice.

SOURCE 26

A teacher and his students at work in a library. The books are neatly stacked on the shelves behind them. All books were carefully copied out by hand. This meant that they were very valuable: there might be only five or ten copies of a book in the whole world.

'When the fire is fanned –
Wood or charcoal –
Flames rise up like cedar trees of gold.'

SOURCE 28

Translation from an Arabic poem by Abdullah Ibn al-Mu'tazz (861–908). Al Mu'tazz was born in the palace city of Samarra in Iraq, and was related to the great caliph, Harun al-Rashid.

'They call me Sinbad the Sailor, and marvel at my strange history . . . Seven voyages I made in all, and each a story of such marvel as . . . fills the soul with wonder.'

SOURCE 29

The beginning of the traditional Muslim story, 'Sinbad the Sailor'.

Popular literature

As many people could not read, they relied on the spoken word for their entertainment. Poetry was enormously popular. Professional storytellers recited poems and humorous stories in the market place and at street corners. They entertained passers-by with stories like the one in Source 27. In return, they would receive gifts of money or food.

A man claimed that he was a prophet. People were suspicious and so they said to him, 'Prove it.'
'That's easy,' replied the false prophet. 'I will tell you what thoughts are passing through your minds.'
'All right, then,' they replied. 'Tell us what we are thinking this very minute.'
The impostor laughed. 'You are thinking that I am a liar, and not a prophet at all,' he said.

SOURCE 27

From a 14th century Persian joke book.

Storytellers and poets were also invited into people's homes to entertain them, particularly on special occasions. They often accompanied their words with music. Muslim rulers invited poets and musicians to live at their courts and entertain them with poems like the one in Source 28.

Many traditional Muslim stories have travelled to the West. They have been used to provide plots for pantomimes and even for films. Among the best known are 'Aladdin', 'Sinbad the Sailor' (see Source 29) and 'Ali Baba and the Forty Thieves'. These stories were probably first told in the 8th and 9th centuries, but were not written down until much later.

Islam and other cultures

During the Middle Ages, Muslim travellers carried their faith further afield, to southern Europe, Africa and Asia (Source 1). These travellers included a number of learned scholars, who were often asked to work for non-Muslim kings and princes.

King Roger of Sicily, a 12th century Christian ruler, employed a famous Muslim geographer, Al-Idrisi, to produce a map of the world, along with a book describing various countries. Al-Idrisi's map was engraved on a huge silver dish. Although his silver map no longer exists, the text of Al-Idrisi's book (see Source 2) and several of his smaller maps, have survived. An example is shown in Source 4. They are very accurate, and far in advance of other maps produced at that time.

AIMS

In this unit we will find out about the continuing spread of Islam. By the 12th century there were Muslims living in almost every part of the known world, from West Africa to China.
We will also see how the Muslim heartlands in the Middle East were shaken by invaders. First, Christian armies attacked from the West during the Crusades. Then pagan Mongol armies attacked from the East. Gradually, the Muslim lands recovered under the leadership of a new Muslim ruling family known as the Ottomans.

SOURCE 1

Routes taken by Muslim travellers in the Middle Ages.

KEY
Main overland routes
Sea routes

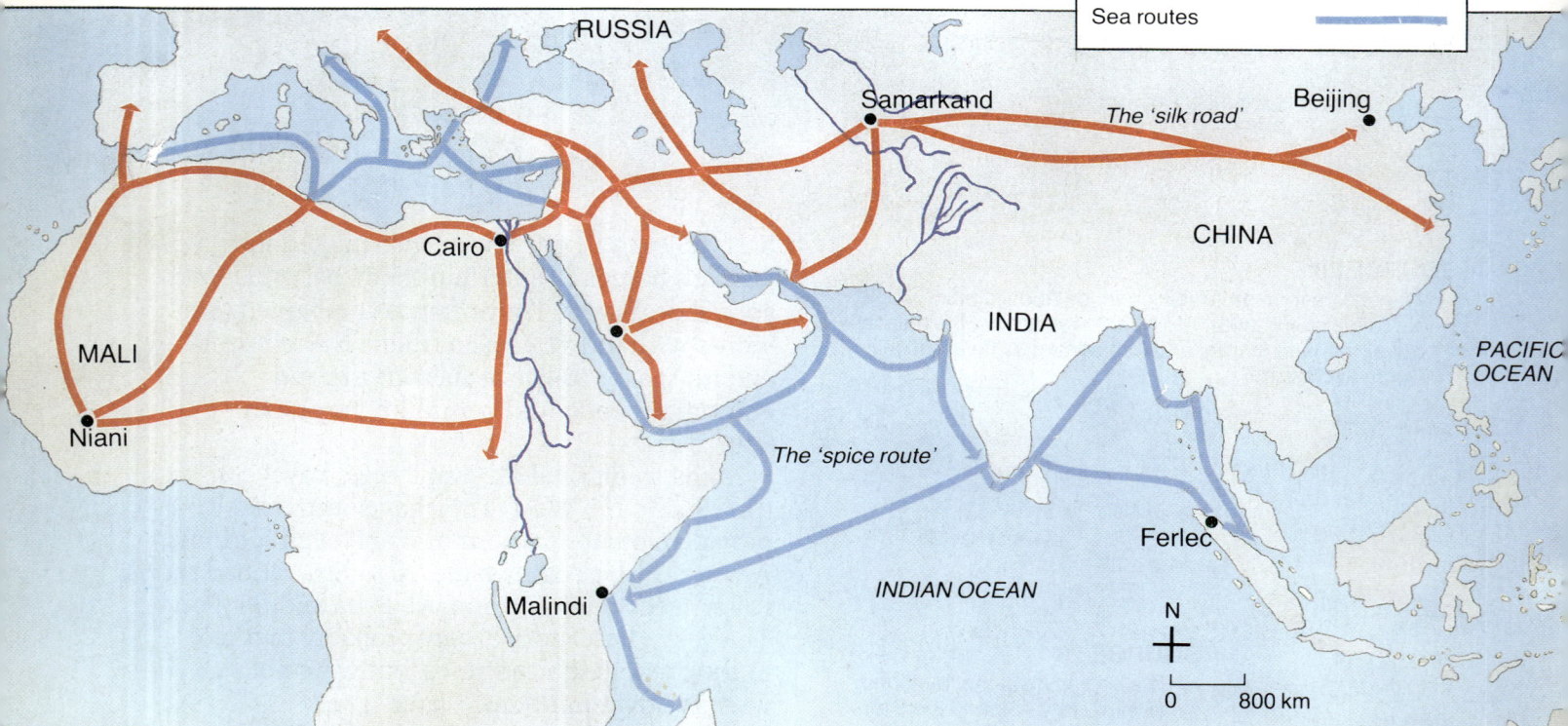

RUSSIA · Samarkand · The 'silk road' · Beijing · CHINA · Cairo · INDIA · PACIFIC OCEAN · MALI · Niani · The 'spice route' · Ferlec · Malindi · INDIAN OCEAN · N · 0 800 km

'The town of Malindi is on the sea shore at the mouth of a sweet water stream. It is a large town and its people live from hunting and fishing. They hunt leopards and wolves and fish in the sea for various fish, which they salt and sell. They work in an iron mine which provides most of their livelihood and trade.'

SOURCE 2
Extract from al-Idrisi's book (late 12th century) describing Malindi, on the coast of present-day Kenya in East Africa (see Source 1).

Travellers' tales

Ibn Battuta was perhaps the most famous of Muslim travellers. On his last journey he visited Mali in West Africa (see Source 1), where the kings were Muslim. He describes the visit in Source 3.

Evidence from another famous traveller, the Italian, Marco Polo, shows how Islam had spread in the East (Source 5). Land and sea trade routes brought Islam to distant lands, and introduced new skills into the Muslim heartlands.

For example, the Arabian sailing ship, or DHOW, in Source 6 used a steering rudder at the back. This was a Chinese invention dating back to the 1st century AD. It was copied by Arabian boat builders and so eventually spread to the West.

SOURCE 4
One of al-Idrisi's smaller maps.

'You must know that the people of Ferlec (an important coastal city in Sumatra) used to be idolaters, but owing to contact with Saracen (Muslim) merchants, who continually visit here in their ships, they have all been converted to the law of Muhammad.'

SOURCE 5
From 'The Travels of Marco Polo', an Italian merchant who lived at the end of the 13th century.

SOURCE 6
This manuscript picture from Baghdad (1238) shows an Arabian dhow.

Use Source 1 to measure these distances: Cairo to China; Mecca to Mali; Malindi to Ferlec. What do these figures tell us about Muslim travellers?

'(The people of Mali) possess some admirable qualities. They are seldom unjust . . . Their Sultan shows no mercy to anyone who is guilty of the least act of it. Neither traveller nor inhabitant in it has anything to fear from robbers or men of violence. They do not confiscate the property of any (Arab) who dies in their country, even if it be uncounted wealth.'

SOURCE 3
Ibn Battuta's description of his visit to Niani, the capital of Mali, in 1353.

- Do not kill a young child, an old man, or a woman.
- Do not destroy palm trees or orchards.
- Do not kill a sheep or a cow or a camel, except for food.
- Do not attack Christian or Muslim monasteries, or places of prayer.

SOURCE 7
Rules of conduct for Muslim soldiers. Such rules were in use during the crusader wars.

SOURCE 8
Manuscript illustration showing the recapture of Jerusalem by Saladin's troops in 1187. Muslim soldiers (in pointed helmets) enter the gates, while the Crusaders fight back from the battlements. Soldiers from both sides wait outside.

Defending Islam

Islam spread into many parts of the world peacefully, through Muslim merchants and other travellers. Sometimes, though, Muslims and non-Muslims came into contact with each other through conflict and war. Source 7 shows how Muslim soldiers were meant to behave in wartime.

The Crusades

The most famous clash between Muslim and Christian forces in the Middle Ages came during the CRUSADES. These were a series of invasions by Christian troops of what they called 'the Holy Land'. This was the territory surrounding the city of Jerusalem. The Crusades lasted for almost 200 years, from 1095 until 1291, with a few final outbreaks of fighting in the 14th and 15th centuries.

When the Christian armies invaded Jerusalem in 1099, the city had been under Muslim rule for over 400 years. In 1187, it was recaptured by Muslim troops as shown in Source 8. This victorious army was led by Saladin, ruler of Egypt and Syria. The Crusader wars dragged on, but Jerusalem remained firmly under Muslim control.

'All those who were well informed about the Franj (the Crusaders) saw them as beasts superior in courage and in eagerness to fight but in nothing else, just as animals are superior in strength and aggression.'

SOURCE 9
From a history of the Crusades written by Usamah ibn Munqidh, a Syrian who lived in the early 12th century. He based his book upon eyewitness accounts.

'. . . this day, I say, marks the justification of all Christianity and the humiliation of paganism; our faith was renewed.'

SOURCE 10
Comment by Raymond of Agiles, a 12th-century historian, on the capture of Jerusalem by the Crusaders.

Some Muslim soldiers were besieging a Christian fortress. This was a massive building, almost like a small town. Several Christians were sheltering inside, including a young couple who had arranged to get married, but whose plans had been stopped by the fighting. They decided to get married anyway, even though they were trapped inside the castle.

The great Muslim general, Saladin, was in charge of the besieging troops. When he heard about the wedding, he ordered his soldiers not to attack the castle where the young couple were staying, so they could enjoy peace and quiet. In return, the bride's mother sent out trays of food, so that Saladin and his troops could share in the wedding celebrations.

SOURCE 11

Traditional story, from Muslim sources.

English	Arabic
Admiral	from *Amir* meaning 'leader' or 'commander'
Apricot	*al-birquq*
Coffee	*qahwah*
Cotton	*qutun*
Jar	*jarrah*
Lemon	*laimun*
Orange	*naranj*
Sherbet	*sarba*, meaning 'drink'
Sugar	*sukkar*

SOURCE 12

The English words for all these things come from Arabic, as you can see. The fruits and other items were introduced to Northern Europe at the time of the Crusades.

Sources 9 and 10 give two different points of view, Christian and Muslim, about the Crusades. For many people on both sides this was a 'holy' war: they were fighting to control a place that they believed was sacred to their faith. But the final results of the Crusades were tragic: the bitterness they caused between the two communities lasted for centuries. Thousands of people on both sides were tortured and killed, often for reasons that had more to do with politics than religion.

There were periods of peace, even in the middle of war. Christian and Muslim soldiers arranged truces. Sometimes they staged mock battles to entertain local children. Crusaders returning home to Europe brought with them many new words and ideas from the Muslim world. Source 12 shows some examples.

SOURCE 13

This portrait of Saladin (1137–93) was painted by an Egyptian artist. In Europe, Saladin is mostly remembered for his success as a military leader. In the Muslim world, he is also remembered as the founder of the Ayyubids, a new ruling family in Egypt.

ACTIVITY

Use Source 11 to write and act out a scene at the siege of a town during the crusader wars. Source 8 shows what the people wore.

The characters are:

- A Christian soldier. He feels he is fighting a 'holy' war (see Source 10).
- The young couple.
- The bride's mother. Find out what food she might offer. (Use Source 12 to help you).
- A soldier in Saladin's army. He might agree with the historian Usamah ibn Munqidh (see Source 9 for his views).

Changes in the Muslim world

From the 10th century onwards, there were many changes in the Muslim world. As we saw earlier, the power of the caliphs in Baghdad was weakened, and a number of Muslim territories broke away from their control. In North Africa for example, Cairo became the new and important capital city for the Fatimid ruling family (see Source 14). The Fatimids governed Egypt and the surrounding territories until 1171 when they were replaced by the great military leader Saladin (see Source 13).

SOURCE 14
One of three magnificent gates to the city of Cairo, built by the Fatimids in the 10th century.

SOURCE 16
This bridge crosses the Horashan River in Turkey. It was built by the Seljuks between the 12th and 15th centuries.

SOURCE 15
This 13th century dish shows a Seljuk archer drawing his bow to shoot, while riding a galloping horse.

In the northern and eastern Muslim states, the Seljuk Turks became a powerful force. They came from Central Asia, and were originally nomads. As they wandered westwards in search of grazing for their flocks and herds, they became converted to Islam.

Source 15 shows that the Seljuks were skilful soldiers, who won positions of power in many Muslim governments. Under the military protection of the Seljuks, many Muslim lands became safer to live and travel in. Roads were improved (see Source 16) and new guest houses were built along main routes.

The widening world of Islam

During the 12th and 13th centuries, Islam spread rapidly. By 1500, many people in West and East Africa had become Muslim (see Sources 17 and 18). King Mansa Musa of Mali was a faithful Muslim and made a grand pilgrimage to Mecca in 1324. However, he and his followers took so much Malian gold with them to sell on their journey that its price dropped by 20 per cent in the Cairo bazaars.

A brilliant Muslim civilisation also grew up in part of present-day Afghanistan. It was centred on the palace of Muhammad of Ghazni who ruled in the early 11th century. Like many other Muslim rulers, he encouraged artists and scholars to live and study at his court. Further south, Muslim sultans ruled over a powerful state in Delhi, founded in 1209. There were also Muslims among the merchant communities living in the great trading cities in China.

The lands in which these new Muslim people lived, their languages, working conditions and local customs were very different. But they were all united as members of the international community of Islam.

SOURCE 17
This map was produced in Muslim Spain in the 14th century. It shows the King of Mali and a Muslim visitor from North Africa.

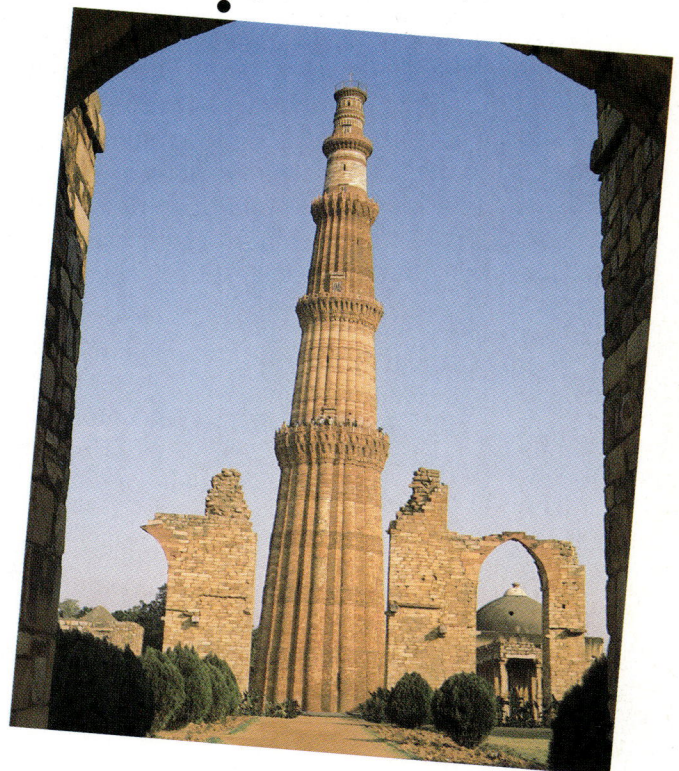

SOURCE 18
Lamu, in present-day Kenya, is one of several East African coastal towns that started life as Muslim settlements and trading posts.

SOURCE 19
Qutb minaret in Delhi, northern India.

The Mongol invasions

As we have seen, there were a number of changes in the Middle East in the 10th and 11th centuries. But in the 13th century, there was a far more dramatic change caused by an invading army of Mongols from Asia. In 1258 they finally reached Baghdad and destroyed most of the city. Those who were not killed fled in terror. Other great Muslim cities were also attacked, and people's homes and crops were destroyed.

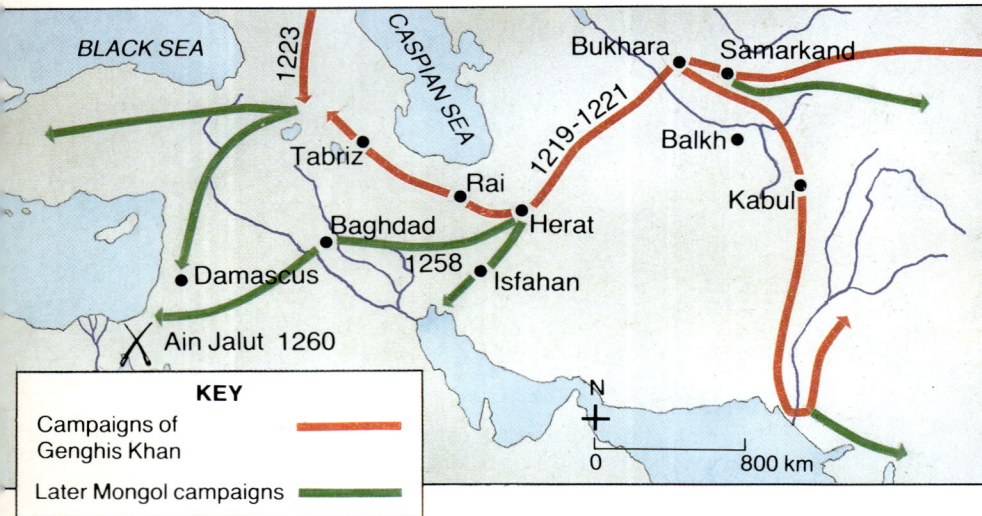

SOURCE 20
Mongol leader Genghis Khan in his richly decorated tent. A 13th century Persian manuscript illustration.

SOURCE 21
Mongol invasions into the Middle East during the 13th century.

Who were the Mongols?

The Mongols were a group of nomadic tribes, who lived in the northern plains of Central and East Asia. In 1206 they were united under the leadership of Genghis Khan (see Source 20). His ambition was to rule over all the known world. Genghis led the Mongol troops on a series of raids westwards towards the Middle East and Europe. Source 21 charts their progress as they swept on horseback into the cities of the Muslim world.

Oh people, know that you have committed great sins . . . If you ask me what proof I have for these words, I say it is because I am the punishment of God. If you had not committed great sins, God would not have sent a punishment like me upon you.

SOURCE 23
Speech by Genghis Khan to the survivors of the Mongol attack on Bukhara in 1220.

The events I shall describe are so horrible that for years I avoided all mention of them. It is not easy to announce that death has fallen upon Islam and the Muslims. I would have preferred my mother never to have given birth to me, or to have died without witnessing these evils . . .
No, probably not until the end of time will a catastrophe of such magnitude be seen again.

SOURCE 22
Comment on the Mongol invasions by Ibn al-Athir (1160-1233), an Arab historian living at the time.

'Ghengis Khan died in China, but left orders that he was to be buried in his homeland of Mongolia. His body was carried hundreds of miles overland, attended by soldiers. They killed every living thing that they passed by, with the words: "Depart for the next world and there attend upon your dead lord." '

SOURCE 24
The story of Genghis Khan's funeral procession, as described by medieval Mongol historians.

SOURCE 25
The dome of Timur's tomb in Samarkand.

SOURCE 26
Comment on one of the reasons for the Mongol armies' behaviour, from a modern history book.

'The truth was that in a medieval army so far from home the loyalty of the soldiers depended on whether their leader could find them enough to plunder. Timur could hardly afford good behaviour on the part of the towns he passed.'

Mongol rule

After Genghis Khan's death, other Mongol leaders continued these invasions until it looked as if the Mongols would indeed rule over the whole world. The last great Mongol leader, Timur (1336 to 1405) became a Muslim, although he did not live in a way that more faithful Muslims could approve. Under his command, Mongol armies continued their fierce attacks on Middle Eastern countries, and marched into India.

However, Timur also encouraged trade, and spent many years rebuilding Samarkand into a beautiful capital city. Sad to say, a lot of this work was carried out by prisoners. Timur took the best craftsmen in all the territories he conquered and forced them to go to Samarkand to produce masterpieces for him.

The results of the Mongol invasions were terrible and long-lasting for many of the countries they entered. But, in 1260 a Muslim army led by Egyptian commanders managed to stop the Mongol advance at the battle of Ain Jalut. This gave the Muslim lands a chance to recover.

SOURCE 27
Comment on the Mongol invasions by a modern American historian.

The effects of the devastation wrought by the Mongols are only now being mended. Millions of people perished; cities vanished; canals silted and irrigation decreased; lands became barren and deserted; government disintegrated; civilisation foundered and life returned to the bare essentials.

attainment target 1

1 How did the Mongol invasions affect:
   - Baghdad
   - Everyday life in Muslim areas
   - Samarkand?

2 What would the effects of a Mongol attack on a town be:
   - In the first few days
   - After six months
   - After 20 years?

3 Look at the results of the Mongol invasions given in Source 27. Which do you think would be the most serious for the people of Muslim lands?

attainment target 2

1 Give one fact and one opinion from Source 27.

2 What different type of information is given in Sources 22 and 27?

3 What kind of evidence has the author of Source 27 used which Ibn al-Athir (Source 22) did not have?

The Ottoman empire

After the Mongols retreated, a number of new Islamic states were established in Turkey, Persia, Iraq and Central Asia. One of the earliest and most successful of these was founded by a local Turkish chieftain, possibly descended from Seljuk nomads. His name was Uthman, often spelled 'Ottoman' in English. Uthman and his successors became the rulers of a mighty Muslim empire, shown in Source 28.

SOURCE 28
The Ottoman empire by 1500.

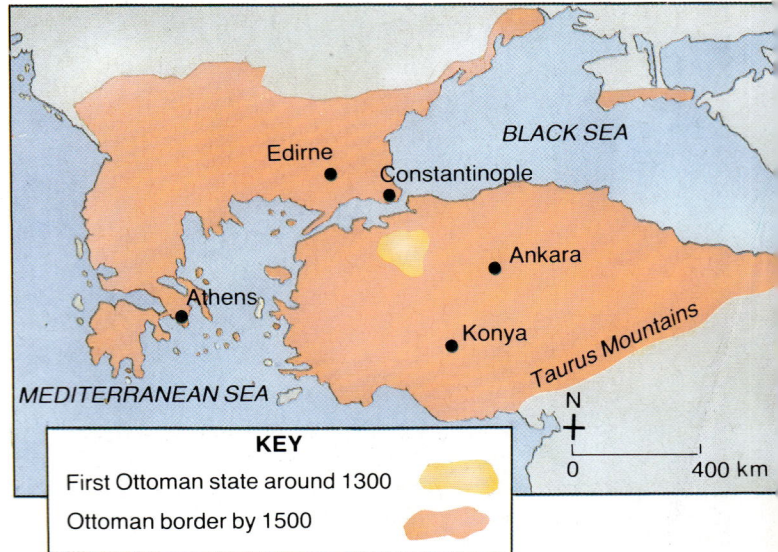

KEY
First Ottoman state around 1300
Ottoman border by 1500

Look at Sources 29 and 30. Read the captions and compare the ways in which people and buildings are drawn and painted. Which picture do you think is more reliable as evidence? Why?

SOURCE 30
Ottoman Sultan Mehmet the Conqueror receiving European visitors in his palace. The picture was painted by the Italian artist Gentile Bellini who visited Constantinople in 1480.

SOURCE 29
The capture of Constantinople by the Ottomans in 1453. From a manuscript produced in France in the second half of the 15th century.

Ottoman victories

Uthman reigned from 1281 to 1324 and the ruling family he founded went on to conquer more territories over the next hundred years. In 1453, Muslim Ottoman troops finally captured the Byzantine capital of Constantinople (present-day Istanbul). You can see the battle scene in Source 29. From now on, the Ottomans were rulers of the most powerful state in the Muslim world. They also controlled the remains of the Byzantine empire, from where they later advanced far into Europe. The Ottoman empire lasted for hundreds of years as a great Muslim power. It finally collapsed in 1924.

Life under the early Ottomans

Not surprisingly, the Ottomans' rise to power created many enemies, in Europe, and among other Muslim states. The Ottoman rulers defended and extended their empire with the help of the latest weapons such as guns and heavy cannon. Instead of raising taxes in captured lands to pay for their troops, the Ottomans took Christian boys and trained them as expert soldiers or JANISSARIES. In this way they built up a skilled, professional army, loyal to the empire.

Like many earlier Muslim rulers, the Ottoman sultans paid for beautiful buildings and works of art (see Source 32). One of the most famous patrons of art and learning was the Ottoman emperor Suleiman the Magnificent. He ruled from 1520 to 1566. During his reign the splendour and magnificence of the Ottomans reached its peak.

SOURCE 31

Text of a carved notice made in Romania in 1533, recording Suleiman's powers.

'I am God's slave and sultan of this world. By the grace of God I am head of Muhammad's community. God's might and Muhammad's miracles are my companions. I am Caliph* in Mecca and Medina. In Baghdad I am the Shah*, in Byzantine realms the Caesar*, and in Egypt the Sultan*; who sends his fleets into the seas of Europe, North Africa and India. I am the Sultan who took the crown and throne of Hungary . . .'

*All these titles are used here to mean 'all-powerful ruler'

SOURCE 32

This mosque at Edirne in Turkey was designed by the Muslim architect Sinan, and built during Suleiman's reign.

ACTIVITY

This is a whole class activity, set at the court of the caliph, in Baghdad in the 9th century. Here are some suggestions for the characters:

THE CALIPH: you must decide what he is like.

COURTIERS AND ADVISERS: some are loyal to the caliph, some just flatter him, and some plot his downfall.

THE CALIPH'S WIFE — THE CALIPH'S MOTHER: they see and listen to all that is going on from behind a screen. The caliph respects their advice.

SCRIBES: they record the caliph's decisions and do beautiful writing.

MERCHANTS: they come from faraway places with exotic goods to sell at court.

TOWNSPEOPLE: they live by trade and rely on the caliph's good government.

ARMY GENERAL: there is trouble in a distant province.

SCHOLARS: experts in all forms of knowledge.

QADIS: judges, expert in Islamic law.

DOCTOR: has knowledge of illnesses and remedies from many civilisations.

ARCHITECT: in charge of new building project.

SERVANTS AND SLAVES: to serve food and drink.

MUSICIANS AND STORYTELLERS: to entertain the court.

AMBASSADOR: arrives with gifts and messages from a distant land.

Various pages in this book contain information that will help you to set the scene and to understand how the characters might act. They are as follows:

The caliph's palace, life at court (31–39).
The teachings of Muhammad (9–15). Many of the characters would know these well, but not everyone would follow them.
How caliphs should govern (20–27).
Trade, the journeys made by merchants and the goods they brought (18–19; 28-29; 36–37; 50–51).
Women at court (35).
Examples of scribes' work (9; 21).
Muslims at war (16–17; 52–53).
The work of a qadi (23).
Townspeople and town life (22–23; 29; 36–37).
Architecture, buildings and crafts (40–43).
Scholars and learning (41; 44–46).
Medicine (45).
Musicians and storytellers (35; 48–49).
Ambassadors (19; 32–33).

Here are some of the things that happen at court:
- The townspeople arrive, complaining about blocked water fountains.
  They ask the caliph to lay on better supplies of water.
- The merchants show off the goods they have to sell.
- The general needs more soldiers and better military equipment to protect a border area from invasion.
- The scholars want to build new extensions for the madrasa.
- The doctor comes to treat the caliph's son who is ill.
- The ambassador wants to open up a trade link between his country and lands governed by the caliph.

The caliph seeks advice and information from various people at the court in order to deal with these situations. His decision then has to be made and recorded. Entertainment is provided and there is a continuous supply of refreshments.

Glossary

Allah
One True God. Muslims believe that there is only one God, the Creator and Sustainer of the universe, who is also worshipped by Christians and Jews. Muslims believe that it is totally wrong to worship any other person, spirit or object.

Archaeologist
Someone who investigates the past by studying the remains of earlier civilisations. These remains can include ruined buildings, objects buried in the soil, graves and tombs, even ancient rubbish pits.

Astrolabe
An instrument used in the Middle Ages to measure the height and position of the stars. It was particularly useful for sailors, navigating their ships while out of sight of land.

Astronomers
Mathematicians and scientists who study the moon and the stars.

Autobiography
The story of someone's life, written by themselves.

Caliph pronounced *'kāylif'*
Ruler of the Islamic peoples. Gods 'deputy' on earth. The caliphs were responsible for seeing that the faith of Islam was protected in their lands. They were also meant to rule according to God's teachings, as reported by Muhammad and recorded in the *Qur'an*.

Converted
Decided to follow a new religion.

Crusades
Wars between Christians and Muslims, fought between the 11th and 13th centuries, mainly in Palestine.

Dhow pronounced to rhyme with *'how'*.
A sailing ship with a large, triangular sail, built to carry cargo between Arabia, India and East Africa.

Hadith
Words spoken by the *Prophet* Muhammad. Hadith were carefully remembered by people who heard Muhammad preach and teach, and passed on by word of mouth from generation to generation. Several centuries after Muhammad's death, hadith were collected and written down by Muslim scholars. Muslims regard hadith with great respect, since they are a record of the advice given to the earliest members of the Muslim community by one of God's prophets.

Hajj
Pilgrimage to Mecca. There are many ceremonies within the hajj. It includes a visit to the *Ka'aba* and other holy places in and around Mecca.

Idols
Objects or images worshipped by people.

Irrigation
Bringing water to dry lands, so that crops may be grown there.

Islam
The worship of the 'One True God'. People who follow the faith of Islam, today as in the past, are known as *Muslims*. Muslims believe that the *Prophet* Muhammad was a messenger sent by God to teach them how to live and how to worship.

Janissary
A specially trained soldier, from a Christian family who fought in the armies of the Muslim rulers of the Ottoman Empire.

Ka'aba pronounced *'Kāāba'*
Specially constructed chamber built to house the sacred Black Stone in the House of Prayer at Mecca.

Kamal pronounced *'ke-māl'*
A simple instrument (made out of a square of wood and a piece of knotted string) which helped sailors to work out their position at sea.

Khan pronounced *'kāān'*
A rest-house for travellers, where they could find food, water and shelter for themselves and their animals.

Madrasa
A college, where Islamic subjects, especially law, could be taught.

Mangonel
A war-machine, rather like a large catapult, which hurled rocks or other heavy objects towards the enemy.

Medieval
Belonging to the Middle Ages – the years around 500 AD to around 1500 AD. The period from around 500 AD to around 1000 AD is sometimes known as 'the Dark Ages', but only for Britain and parts of Europe. In Spain and many parts of the Middle East great Muslim civilisations flourished in this period.

Mosque
A building where Muslims meet and listen to sermons.

Muslim
Someone who follows the faith of Islam. Muslims worship *Allah* – the One True God – and try to live according to the teachings of the Qur'an and the example set by Muhammad.

Naphtha
An explosive mixture, used by Muslim troops to set fire to enemy ships or buildings during the *Middle Ages.* It could not be put out by pouring water on the flames, only by smothering the fire with vinegar.

Nomad
Someone who lives a wandering life, moving from place to place, usually looking after large flocks and herds of sheep, goats, camels or other animals.

Observatory
A building where *astronomers* go to study the moon and the stars.

Patron
A wealthy person who gives money to pay for a work of art, architecture or scholarship.

Pilgrimage
A journey to a holy shrine or holy place.

Prophet
A (human) messenger sent by God to teach people the right way to live. Muslims believe that there have been many prophets throughout the centuries, but that now there will be no more prophets after Muhammad.

Qadi pronounced *'kādi'*
An Islamic judge, learned in Islamic law.

Qanat pronounced *'kenāt'*
A system of wells, designed to bring water to dry areas.

Qur'an pronounced *'kurān'*
A book containing the message sent by God and received by Muhammad, written down shortly after Muhammad died. Muslims believe that the Qur'an contained precise instructions from God, telling them how to live.

Ramadan
The ninth month of the Islamic calendar. In Ramadan, Muslims fast (take no food or drink) during daylight hours. They believe that this self-discipline helps to bring them closer to God.

Scribe
A specially-trained person who made a living reading and writing documents for people who were unable to do so themselves. Some scribes specialised in producing particularly beautiful manuscripts.

Shari'ah
Islamic law, based on the teachings of the *Qur'an.* It was used in Medieval Islamic countries to govern all aspects of peoples' lives.

Shi'ite pronounced *'shēē-ite'*
One of the two major groups within the Muslim community.

Souk pronounced *'sook'*
Market-place in Muslim countries. Traditional street markets or covered markets are an important feature of Muslim towns and cities.

Sunni pronounced *'sōōni'*
The other major group within the Muslim community (see *Shi'ite*, above).

Superpowers
Very powerful countries.

Textiles
Various kinds of woven cloth, including carpets.

Toll
Tax paid for use of a market, or public road.

Index

Page numbers in **bold** refer to illustrations/captions

First published 1991 by CollinsEducational
77-85 Fulham Palace Road
Hammersmith
London W6 8JB

ISBN-0-00-327231-1

Cover designed by Glynis Edwards
Book designed by Julia Osorno
Edited by Charlotte Rolfe and Nicole Lagneau
Picture research by Suzanne Williams
Artwork by Julia Osorno
Production by Mandy Inness

Typeset by Dorchester Typesetting Group Ltd.

Printed and bound by Stige-Arti Grafiche, Italy

Acknowledgements

Every effort has been made to contact the holders of copyright material but if any have been inadvertently overlooked the publishers will be pleased to make the necessary arrangements at the first opportunity.

Photographs The publishers would like to thank the following for permission to reproduce photographs on these pages:

T = top, B = bottom, R = right, C = centre, L = left

Alinari 6R; Ancient Art & Architecture Collection 30L; Bibliothèque Nationale, Paris 23B; Bodleian Library, Oxford 51T; British Library Board 17L; British Museum 18T, 29T, 54B; Camerapix Picture Library 8L, 11TB; Chester Beatty Library Dublin 33; Jean Dieuzaide, Toulouse 52; E.T. Archive 9R, 41T/Victoria & Albert Museum; Edinburgh University Library 19, 20, 46; Giraudon 6L/Private Collection, New York, 26B/ Louvre, Paris; Sonia Halliday Photographs/ Bibliothèque Nationale, Paris 18C, 22, 31, 32TB, 35, 37T, 49, 51B, 59, 58L; The Robert Harding Picture Library 7R, 13/Freer Gallery of Art, Washington, 18BL, 26T, 29L & BR/British Library, 30R, 38T, 40, 41B, 43, 44/University Library, Istanbul, 47T, 54C, 55T, 55BL, 57T; Hirmer Fotoarchiv 36L; Michael Holford 37B, 47B, 55BR; The Hutchinson Library 7L, 14, 24, 38B, 42T; A.F. Kersting 54T; Lauros Giraudon 58R; Roget-Viollet 23; Screen Ventures 10, 15; Victoria & Albert Museum 25T; Kunsthistorisches Museum, Vienna 36; Bild-Archiv der Osterreichische Nationalbibliothek, Vienna 17, 21; Wiedenfeld & Nicolson Archives 12, 25B/ Burgerbibliothek, Bern, 42B, 53/Freer Art Gallery, Washington; Werner Forman Archive 9L, 28, 45T/ Metropolitan Museum, New York, 45B/Victoria & Albert Museum, 48, 53.

Cover Photograph: Sonia Halliday Photographs Unit motifs: *Islamic Designs* by Eva Wilson, British Museum, Publication, 1989.

The author and publishers gratefully acknowledge the following publications from which written sources in this book are drawn:

McGraw Hill for an extract from S.N. Fisher and W. Oschenwald, *The Middle East – a history*, 4th edition, 1990; Jonathan Cape for an extract from B. Gascoigne, *The Great Moghuls*, 1971; The International Islamic Foundation of Student Organizations for four hadiths from An-Nawawi's Forty Hadiths, translated by Ezzedin Ibrahim and Denys Johnson-Davies, 2nd edition; Penguin Books for a poem by Abdullah Ibn al-Mu'tazz in G.B. Wightman and A.Y. al-Udhari (trans.) *Birds through a Ceiling of Alabaster*, Penguin, 1975; an extract from R. Latham (ed.) *The Travels of Marco Polo*, 1958; an extract from N.J. Dawood (trans.) *Tales from the Thousand and One Nights*, 1954; Oxford University Press for extracts from B. Lewis (ed. and trans.) *Islam, from the Prophet Muhammad to the Capture of Constantinople*, OUP, 1987, Volume I: Politics and War, Volume II: Religion and Society; Cambridge Educational for extracts from D. Townson, *Muslim Spain*, CUP, 1986; Qur'an quotes from Kenneth Cragg (selected and translated) *Readings in the Qur'an*, Collins Liturgical, 1988 © Professor Kenneth, Cragg, extracts from *The Times – The World an Illustrated History*, Channel 4/Times Books, 1986; an extract from Charis Waddy, *Women in Muslim History*, Longman, 1980; an extract from *The History of the Arabs*, 10th ed., 1970, Philip Hitti, Macmillan Education, © Philip K. Hitti.

We would also like to thank the IQRA Trust for supplying the author with much useful information and for helpful discussions.